Letters from an English Rancher

Letters from an English Rancher

BY CLAUDE GARDINER

edited and introduction

By

Hugh A. Dempsey

Glenbow Museum
130 – 9th Avenue S.W.
Calgary, Alberta, T2G 0P3

Made in Canada

Introduction

In 1894, a twenty-three-year-old Englishman named Claude Gardiner left his home in London for "a situation on a Ranch."[1] During the next two years, he wrote a series of letters to his parents and sister, giving his impressions of ranch life in the foothills of Alberta. These include refreshing and chatty accounts of ranch experiences, presented in simple yet graphic terms for the benefit of a family which had no idea of life in western Canada. As such, they offer a unique look at ranch life in the nineteenth century.

Claude William Edward Gardiner was born on October 17, 1870, the only son of Lt. Col. and Mrs. Edward James Gardiner, of London, England. Both of Claude's grandfathers were men of distinction. His paternal grandfather, William James Gardiner, was an architect of the firm Gardiner & Theobold of London, and was still alive when the young man set out for Canada. He passed away two years later, but not before he had provided assistance to the young emigrant. Claude's maternal grandfather was Dr. Hugh Statham of London, a well known physician.

Claude attended good schools in London and later he worked on his grandfather's estate in Worcester Park, Surrey. There he began to work with horses and enjoyed the outdoor life. After receiving his education, Claude decided that he did not want to follow in the architectural footsteps of his father and grandfather. Instead, he took a position with Alphonse Oarall, wholesalers of woollen goods, and soon became their export manager. When he was twenty-two he joined the

Queen's Westminster Volunteers, rising to the rank of lance corporal. This regiment provided the opportunity for him to pursue his love for horseback riding.

During this time, Gardiner was advised to follow an outdoor life for health reasons. He decided to go farming but he found that the opportunities in Britain were limited. As he explained, "I should only be able to take a very small farm and I should not be able to better myself."[2] At this time, he happened to attend a meeting where the guest speaker was Sir Charles Tupper, High Commissioner for Canada in London and later the nation's Prime Minister. Impressed by the opportunities which Tupper said were available in Canada, the young man began to consider establishing a farm "in the colonies."

At this point, his father wrote to an old friend, Clarence C. Chipman, Chief Commissioner of the Hudson's Bay Company in Winnipeg, asking about the prospects in western Canada. Chipman was in charge of all company business in the West and travelled extensively through the region. He suggested that young Gardiner seek employment on a cattle ranch and, if the business suited him, he might consider buying his own spread.

> If you will arrange for your son to reach Winnipeg about the 1st June, I will be able to place him on a Ranche as promised . . . He must be prepared for long hours and pretty heavy work. He cannot expect to do more than pay his way for some time to come, but this he should do without assistance from home. He will be able to see the country and become acquainted with the conditions of life, and the future will remain with himself.[3]

Although Chipman had met young Claude once briefly in London, he was concerned that the man may turn out to be another of those foppish young Englishmen who were giving other immigrants a bad name. Unwilling to adapt to the conditions of the West, they were the ones who caused employers to post signs, "No Englishmen need apply." Young Gardiner proved to be just the opposite. In fact, he himself made comments in his letters about useless Englishmen who bought ranches and spent their time racing and playing polo. He said they were the laughing stock of the community.

Gardiner was different. He did not drink or swear, and had such high moral principles that he was sometimes in conflict with other members of his family when he disagreed with their actions. He was quiet and reserved yet always enjoyed a small circle of close companions.

Commissioner Chipman contacted his agent at Fort Macleod, Edward F. Gigot, who had lived in the town for eleven years and did business with most of the ranchers. He made arrangements for Gardiner to spend a year with James W. Bell, an ex-Mounted Policeman and one of the most successful old-time ranchers in the district. Besides owning a house in town, Bell had a ranch to the south-east on the Belly River near Slideout and a second one south-west of the town on the Waterton River.

Bell had come west in the 1870s as a member of the North-West Mounted Police. About 1879 he had taken his discharge and, with another ex-policeman named Robert Patterson, he had started a ranch south-east of the town. In 1880 they brought the first of the large herds into southern Alberta and soon had 140 head grazing on the land recently vacated by the buffalo. His partner went on to become a Member of the Legislative Assembly for Alberta, but Bell remained a grassroots rancher until his death in 1902.

Gardiner's wages were £2 per month plus room and board. This was a generous allowance for a green Englishman, particularly during the winter months when many men were glad to exchange their labours for nothing more than an assurance of food and lodgings. One might suspect that the powerful Hudson's Bay Company—merchants, bankers, and real estate dealers—may have had more than a passing influence with rancher Bell.

Gardiner's letters begin on the boat in April of 1894, just after he had left his parents at the docks. Upon arrival in Winnipeg, he presented himself to Chipman, who told the young man that he had a year's engagement with Bell near "MacCloud."

Proceeding west, Gardiner arrived at Fort Macleod, where he was impressed by the Mounted Police, whom he compared to the British Dragoons, by the fact that everyone in the town used telephones, and that the mosquitoes were eating him alive. Thus began his adventures in the West.

Armed with £1,000 for investment purposes, he had a year to decide whether or not he should enter the ranching business. And if he did, he hoped to make his fortune in a few years —perhaps doubling his investment in two years—and then buying a large farm in England. It would, he told his mother, be "nearer to London than Dorset," where he had previously worked.[4]

During the period of these letters, April 1894 to April 1896,

Gardiner provides a regular ongoing account of his experiences in the West. He explains how roundups functioned, describes an early rodeo, tells of the food he ate, the dishes he used, and what it was like to be a lowly ranch hand in a strange land.

These letters, besides being newsy and charming, are important documents of history, for they provide the interesting little details of ranch life that are missing from official reports, reminiscences, and newspapers of the period. Who, for example, would bother to describe his winter clothing:

> I wear a cap that comes over my ears, a pair of overalls as well as trousers, German socks instead of boots, and rubber overshoes that come as high as an ordinary boot, and mitts on my hands. Mitts are very thick woolen gloves with all the fingers in one.[5]

A westerner wouldn't describe such detail, as everyone knew about winter clothing, but these kinds of facts were interesting to an English family back home.

The final weeks of Gardiner's letters are occupied with forthcoming visit of his mother and his sister Barbara. Finally, the May 29, 1896 issue of the *Macleod Gazette* carried the following announcement:

> Mrs. and Miss Gardiner arrived out from England by Wednesday's train, on a 6-mos. visit to Mr. C.W.E. Gardiner, of the Porcupine Hills.

The visit was pleasant for the two women, with Barbara beginning a collection of Indian artifacts and taking photographs whenever they left the ranch. Claude enjoyed having his family with him and any homesickness which he had experienced disappeared forever. The two women also fell in love with the West and remained there until 1902, at which time they went back to England for the funeral of Dr. Statham, Claude's grandfather.

They returned a short time later and purchased a house in Fort Macleod where they lived until 1913, Then, on another trip to England, the war intervened with their planned return to Canada so they settled temporarily in Bournemouth. At the end of the conflict they decided to stay in England.

Meanwhile, Claude met Alice Millicent Edwards, a member of a prominent Canadian family. Her father, Oliver Cromwell Edwards, had been raised in Montreal and had become a medical doctor while his brother, William C. Edwards, went on to become a wealthy industrialist and a member of the Senate of Canada.

In 1882, O.C. Edwards was appointed as medical doctor for the Department of Indian Affairs and, after serving in Qu'Appelle and Regina, he returned east to go into private practice in Ottawa and Montreal. During this time, he was given the opportunity to go as medical officer with treaty paying expeditions to the north on three separate occasions, travelling into the Peace River and Mackenzie River regions. In 1902, he was transferred to the position of medical officer for the Blood and Peigan reserves in southern Alberta.

His wife, Henrietta Muir Edwards, was one of the "famous five" Alberta women who successfully changed the interpretation of the British North America Act. Their appeal resulted in the word "person" in the Act being defined to mean "woman" as well as "man" and accordingly forced the Canadian government to admit women to the Senate and to allow them to hold various other offices. For thirty-five years Mrs. Edwards was the convenor of a standing committee on laws affecting women and children, a group formed by the National Council of Women, and was directly responsible for changes in legislation to better the conditions of women and children.

Shortly after the arrival of the Edwardses to Fort Macleod, their daughter Alice received a temporary position at the Peigan Indian agency, which was only a short distance from Claude Gardiner's ranch. The two met at a Masonic ball early in 1902, fell in love, and were married in January of 1907. For the next quarter century, their home was the Wineglass Ranch, a name selected by Gardiner to replace the name of Springfield Ranch which had been used by the former owners. The couple had two children, Claudia who was born in 1907 and Oliver, born in 1910. Both were born in Dr. Edwards' hospital on the Blood Reserve.

Gardiner specialized in purebred Shorthorn cattle and always had a good herd of horses. His brand was the "Wineglass" for his cattle and the "G 7 Connected" for the horses. Although he never became wealthy at ranching, he had a good life, gradually expanding his holdings from his original land on the north-east quarter of section 16, township 9, range 28, west of the 4th meridian. This was on Olsen Creek immediately north of the Peigan Indian Reserve and fifteen miles due west of Fort Macleod. In 1900 he added the south-east quarter and two years later he bought the south-east quarter of section 15. In

1903 he purchased the south-east quarter of section 21 and then added the north-east quarter of section 15 and part of the south-east quarter of section 22 in 1910. This gave him almost a section and a half of land in one of the finest ranching areas in Alberta.

He loved horses and took great pride in his matched teams that he used for his democrat. Even when motor cars became common, he disdained their use and still relied on his horses.

Besides his love for the ranch, Gardiner had a number of other interests. He applied for a post office in 1905 and when he was accepted, he opened the Olsen Creek office in his ranch. In 1894, he joined the Masonic Lodge in Fort Macleod and over the years he took an active role in their work, ultimately becoming Deputy District Grand Master of the Grand Lodge of Alberta. An Anglican, he also was a warden for Christ Church.

His hobbies were stamp collecting and shooting prairie chickens. He was not a gregarious man, but when he got together with friends he was very animated and a first rate story teller. His relationship with Indians from the Peigan Reserve was amicable and he frequently hired men to help on roundups or at branding time. The Peigans gave him the name *Spitah*, or Tall One, while his wife was *Apotoyaki* or Weasel Tail Woman.

With the outbreak of war in 1914, Gardiner attempted to join the Canadian army but was turned down because he had flat feet. He believed that this condition had been caused by his habit of wearing Indian moccasins around the ranch. Later during the war, three of his cousins were killed in the conflict, so he became more anxious to get overseas and play his part. In 1918, he saved enough money to make his own way to England, where he tried to enlist in the British army. There he was turned down because at the age of forty-eight, he was considered to be too old.

Undaunted, he looked for other ways of serving the Allied cause and in late 1918 he became a volunteer driver for the British Ambulance Committee of the French Red Cross. Although the committee was centred in England, all volunteers were under French military regulations and wore French uniforms. Gardiner was sent to Metz after the armistice and helped evacuate wounded until early in 1919. For this he received a medal and a citation from the French government.

In 1921, the fortunes of the Gardiner family changed when Alice's uncle died in Ottawa. Besides being a senator, William Edwards had been a well-to-do lumberman and industrialist.

He had been president of Canada Cement Co., owned sawmills at Rockland and New Edinburgh, and had been a noted stock breeder and agriculturalist. Shortly before his death he had helped organize a $60 million merger involving a major pulp and paper manufacturer.

In his will, Edwards decreed that his estate be divided equally among ten heirs or their issue; one of the heirs was his brother Oliver. However, the doctor had predeceased the senator, so his share was divided among his three children— college professor Muir Edwards, Margaret Stuart, and Alice Gardiner. The bequest left the Gardiners in a comfortable position for the rest of their lives. They also inherited a summer cottage on the Ottawa River, close to where Alice's father had been born.

The Gardiners made a number of winter trips to Europe, meeting Barbara and her mother on the Italian Riviera and then travelling leisurely to the French Riviera for their holidays. Other winters were spent in Victoria where they both liked the climate and Claude in particular was enchanted by the British influences of the west coast city.

About 1935, Claude decided to settle permanently in Victoria. He always retained a lively interest in southern Alberta, often visiting with old cronies who had also chosen to retire to the west coast. He died in Victoria on December 20, 1942, at the age of seventy-two.

Claude Gardiner's letters were found in his sister's English home after her death in 1960. His daughter, Mrs. Claudia Whipple, rescued them from a trunk in the yard when closing down the house prior to its sale. She brought the letters back to Canada and made a transcript of them. The location of the original letters currently is unknown. In 1986, the transcripts were part of a collection, along with a number of artifacts, which were obtained by the Glenbow Museum from O.E. "Gard" Gardiner, the author's son. Some minor editing was done, particularly to remove extraneous material relating to family matters in the Old Country, to tighten up the text, and to add punctuation, paragraphs, etc. No rewriting or major changes were made in the text, as Gardiner's own words needed no embellishment or alteration.

HUGH A. DEMPSEY

NOTES

1. Letter, Connie Statham to G.S. Statham, Stonewall, Man., May 10, 1894. Gardiner Papers, Glenbow Archives.
2. Letter, Gardiner to his father, December 6, 1894.
3. Letter, C.C. Chipman to E.J. Gardiner, April 2, 1894.
4. Letter, Gardiner to his mother, ca. mid-December 1894.
5. Letter, Gardiner to his mother, ca. November 1894.

Steamship Carthaginian
[April, 1894]

Dear Father,
    I am writing this on Sunday in the saloon and will finish it when we get to Newfoundland sometime on Wednesday. When I left Mother we went down the docks out into the river. It was very nice; we saw all the ships in the docks. It is quite a long journey down through them. When we were out in the river we had lunch. I made a very good one as I expected I should not get another chance for a bit. I kept very well till about 5 when we got out into the sea when I began to be sick. I could not go down to dinner so I stopped on deck till the evening when I went and laid down on the seats on top of the companion way. I felt better by bedtime when I went below and got into my berth.
    Next morning the sea was worse. I tried breakfast but could not manage much and went on deck and got rid of what I did eat. It was quite a little storm all day . I did not do much but lie on my back on a seat; as long as I laid down I was all right but as soon as I got up I was sick. Mrs. Hiley was very kind and brought me some sandwiches and biscuits. I kept on like that till Thursday night when I managed a bit of dinner and have been as fit as anything since. It has been very calm since Friday but there is always a roll on the ship; it makes it very difficult to write. They have taken the fiddles off the table now so it is not bad.
    The ladies have shown up a bit now but for several days Mrs. Hiley was the only one that was about. Everyone was ill more or less. I am enjoying the voyage very much now and eat tremendously. We have several very nice people on board but we are a very quiet lot. There is a Roman Catholic brother on

board, a very jolly man; three other middle-aged men; 2 young officers going out to their regiments in Halifax and Bermuda; and 2 very nice young fellows who are in my cabin. One of then changed places with the sergeant who was in it when I came on board; I don't know how he came to be in the room at all. There is a boy in our room. He is a nuisance to us as he suffers from asthma, poor chap, and has to smoke some beastly stuff sometimes to get his breath and it nearly suffocates us with the smoke. We play games in the day time, quoits and a game called shuffle board. We also of course have a sweep on the run every day. She is an awful slow boat, averaging about 250 miles a day. I don't care how long she takes, I am quite comfortable as long as the sea does not get rough again. I hope it won't but the table seems to move up and down more now than it did when I came down. We do not see much of the officers of the ship. They are very hard worked; when they are not on the bridge they have to sleep as there are only 2 lots on duty. The others are off 4 hours apiece. (At St. John's one told me he had been up for 36 hours because of looking out for ice).

I have not wanted my black coat; we never wear them for dinner. Tell Mother she must not worry about my not having a deck chair as I have not wanted one at all since I came on board. We are rather anxious to see if we get into St. John's as the boat before us could not because of the ice; we shall be the first boat in if we get there. I think I shall stop writing for a bit and go and get some fresh air as the table does not show any signs of being steadier. This is a rotten ship for books, nothing but bibles on board, good books but not light reading. The captain is not a bad sort of old man.

Later. We have just got into St. John's. We were up at 1/2 past 4 to see the ship go in. It has the most narrow entrance of any harbour in the world. There is a good bit of ice in the harbour but it is all broken up so we had no trouble to get in. We passed some icebergs in the night; I saw a small one this morning. I should like to see a big one. St. John's was burnt down a few years ago so it is a newly built town. They go in for seal fishing here and all kinds of fishing besides. The sealing boats are in the harbour now; there is a Man of War in the harbour also but not a big one. I am going on shore after breakfast and will post this letter then. We have a lot of passengers going off here. I hope they will not put any more in our cabin; we get rid of 2 here so we shall be comfortable if they don't.

I think I must finish now as I hear the breakfast going on

and I am as hungry as anything. We have got here a day before they expected us. We had to stop on Sunday for an hour, something was wrong with the engine, otherwise we have had a very good passage. We have seen nothing since we left England till now, not a ship or anything.

Will write in the train or from Halifax.

P.S. After all, I find that if I post this at St. John's it will come on with us to Halifax so I shall post it there. I thought the mail called here on the way home but it does not. St. John's is a very funny town, all wood houses painted different colours and telegraph poles everywhere. The roads are awful, all mud and no macadam at all.

Halifax, Saturday — I have got as far as here all right. Will write again in the train. Had a splendid voyage.

St. John, N.B.,
May 20, 1894

Dear Father,

As you can see I am now at St. John. I left Halifax yesterday and, as trains are not allowed through the State of Maine on Sunday, we have to stop in the station here. I slept last night in the sleeping car. I get to Winnipeg on Thursday. We stopped all day at St. John's, Newfoundland, last Wednesday. I never saw such a wretched town. It was burnt down a short time ago so it does not look so well as it might. There is no attempt to pave the streets and all the houses are built of wood and painted different colours. The Hileys may have to stop there for from 2 to 10 days; it depends on the ice. They did not seem very happy over it.

We got into Halifax on Friday about 8. I went on shore then with my friend Huntsman who came over in my cabin. We went to a hotel in the town. He left early on Saturday morning. It was a very cheap hotel, bed breakfast and dinner for £1.75, no tips to anyone in the hotel. The dinners here are very amusing. You have about 7 or 8 little plates with different mixtures; some are nice but most are very peculiar. Halifax is rather a nice town, nice streets and plenty of people. I left there at 1.20. There were 2 young fellows, brothers, in the train who came over by the same steamer 2nd class. One got off at a junction before this and the other is going on part of the way to Montreal. There was one other on the sleeper with me last night; he is the U.S. immigration agent. He had to go to Halifax to see one of these brothers to give him a certificate to enable him to go into the States. This agent and I are going about together today. He is going on to Montreal. We have to go into the town to get our meals today as there are not any served on the train.

This is a nice town on the sea coast; it is situated at the end of the Bay of Fundy. The time is very confusing here as the trains run on standard time and the time of the town is sun time. The rail time is changed three times in crossing the continent. I shall have about 4 hours to wait at Montreal so I think I shall post this letter there. The sleeping car is a very grand affair but there is only us 2 passengers in it. I expect we shall have a lot more at Montreal. The railroad agent has telegraphed to reserve me a good berth at Montreal where I change trains. The country all along to here is nothing but woods.

I have just had dinner at this hotel. We leave here at 10:20 tonight. My friend Huntsman has gone to a place called Pictou where he lives. He is the son of an English parson and is a civil engineer. It is much warmer here than it was coming along but everything is very backward. There are no leaves on the trees yet. I saw snow in Newfoundland. I went for a drive there with a friend who lives there and in one place the snow was across the road. He had a nice horse and trap, one of the American buggies. Last winter was the worst they have had for years. I think I shall leave off now till we get to Montreal.

H.B. House,
Friday May 25th, 1894

Dear Father,

I am now at Winnipeg and am writing this in Mr. Chipman's drawing room.[1] I had no time to finish this letter at Montreal as I intended and coming along in the train it shook so much I could not write. I had a very nice journey and enjoyed it very much. There is not much to see in the train; it is nothing but forest all the way here. I was met at the station by one of Mr. Chipman's clerks (a Mr. Tremain, a very nice chap) as Mr. Chipman was away all day. Tremain and I went about all day together. We went for a bathe in the river and for a paddle in his

Canadian canoe. We met some friends of his on the river and went and had a picnic lunch with them. Yesterday being the Queen's birthday is kept as a holiday over here; nothing but fireworks all day. I came over to Mr. Chipman's in the evening. We had supper and then went to bed. This morning I went out in the town and over to the Hudson's Bay store. They have a very nice shop and store here and all the head offices are here.

Mr. Chipman has got me a berth on a ranch at a place called MacCloud; it is to the south of Calgary near the border of the States. I get my board and lodging and £2 a month. I do not know yet what day I go on there but I shall know soon; it will be in a day or two. You need not trouble about labels in this country. They use the baggage checking system. You don't have to bother about your luggage at all; you have a metal number for each thing and you cannot get your luggage without the number.

---

c/o J. Bell, Esq.,
Macleod, Alberta
May 30, 1894

Dear Father,
The above is my address. I have just got to my journey's end and am writing this letter at once as I do not know when I shall have time to write another. I have just been introduced to my boss Mr. J. Bell and he is gone down to see about some things for the roundup. We start tomorrow or the day after and go right away for a fortnight or more. I shall be in the saddle all day on the day herd; it is the easiest job or rather easier than the night herd. I have only spoken to the boss for a few minutes so cannot say much about him yet but he seems a nice sort of man. I will write more at the end of this letter if I get time when he comes back.

I stopped with Mr. Chipman till Monday. Mr. and Mrs. Chipman were very kind to me. I enjoyed my stay there very much. They thought me looking a lot better than when they saw me in London. I have had a good bit of railway travelling now as I did not get here until 1 o'clock and I left Winnipeg at 1/2 past 9 in the morning on Monday. The fare here was rather dear, $39.25 about £8. The cost of living on the train is not very much; it is 75 cents a meal and they are very good meals too. I had 17 meals on the train. I stopped for a few hours at Calgary last night as the train got there at 1 in the morning and the one here did not start till 7.30 so I went to a hotel to bed and had breakfast there. It is very nice in the train; I do not find it at all tiring. I spent a good bit of my time on the back platform of the car; you get a very good view and plenty of air there. I met some very decent people in the train and so the time passed pleasantly enough.

I am within the sight of the Rocky Mountains and can see the snow in them. The view from the train coming here is not much; all the way to Winnipeg you go through nothing but pine forests and after that you hardly see a tree. The prairie is not so flat as people say, at least as I thought it was it is full of small hills and valleys. The worst thing out here is the mosquitoes; I am eaten up with them. I counted 50 bites on my right hand. This place is a funny little town, or rather you would call it a village, all wooden houses. I do not know yet how many miles from here I shall live as Mr. Bell has 2 ranches.[2] They have a telephone here as they do everywhere out here. At the Chipman's the telephone seemed to be going all day long. Mrs. Chipman does all her shopping by it and speaks to all her friends by it. I even heard one of the little boys use it to ask the time by. It seems very amusing to hear them.

This place is full of the Mounted Police; they have a large place here, nearly 200 men, I think. They are a fine lot of men. Their uniform is very like a dragoon's—a scarlet coat, dark blue breeches with a yellow stripe, and a forage cap with a yellow band round it. They carry a revolver in a belt stuck full of cartridges. I saw several Indians coming along; there are several reservations close to here. They are not a bad looking lot but they smell terribly. It is very hot today. I shall be glad to get into my summer things.

I am glad I don't have to cross the Rockies now as the line is blocked in several places. The snow melting on the mountains causes the earth to slide down on the line and in one place a bridge was carried away. The name of this place is pronounced Macloud; that is why I spelt it wrong in my last letter. I believe that there is a paper in London called the Weekly Telegraph. If there is and it is a good weekly paper, I should like to see it. Do not trouble to send the Telegraph if it is not up to much but I was told it was published by the Daily Telegraph and was rather a good paper. The train comes here twice a week on Wednesdays and Saturdays and returns the same day so you do not have to bother about the timetable much.

I have just been to tea with Mr. Bell. He is married but they are living in the town now because of the children. I do not know whether they will go out to the ranch or not after the roundup. I shall know much more next time I write. The place is full of cowboys now. My work will be to look after the riding horses in the day time and to help the cook. I have had to buy a pair of boots and a hat and gloves. I must finish now as I must get into bed.

Belleview Ranch,
Macleod, Alberta,
June 17, 1894

Dear Mother,

At last I have come into the town again and can write to you. I got in last night. I have got on all right so far. We started out for the roundup just after my last letter to you was written and went out about 8 miles and camped. I had to look after the horses till 9 o'clock at night, nothing to do only to ride about them and see that they did not stray away or get mixed with any others. At night another man took them on. We slept in a tent on the ground. I slept in the same bed with Bell as I had no bedding. We got up before 4 in the morning and cooked breakfast. When that was over the horses were driven in to the wagons and the men caught what saddle horses they wanted. I saddled the horse I was going to ride and took over the others for the rest of the day. That would be about 5 o'clock and I had them till 9 at night, a good long day's work. I had to drive them in when the men came to camp for dinner and take charge of the horses that they had been riding. They would catch fresh ones for the afternoon and finish about 5 or 6 in the evening.

When we shifted camp, I had to drive the horses along behind the wagon. It was rather a sight to see us move camp. There were three other outfits besides us and we used to make a regular procession. First came the wagon, then the horses of that outfit, then another wagon and a lot of horses, and so on. It was rather hard to keep the horses from getting mixed as there would be about 400 altogether on the way at once. I had about 50 in my lot but the others had over 100 each. Each outfit represented a different part of the country. Ours was the lot from the Slideout. There were 5 in our lot and a man to night herd and myself day herd. Then there was the Pincher Creek outfit with all the men from that end of the range, and another lot from another part with the Cockeron Ranch outfit.[3] The Cockeron ranch is a large ranch company near here; they own about 8000 cattle. There was a young Englishman day herding for them, a very nice fellow who had been to the school at Epsom. His name is Kenard, a doctor's son.[4] He had been out in America for 5 years and had saved a little money but not enough to start him yet.

I took to the living at once. You had to eat everything off the same plate, a tin one. I was told we did not live as well as some of the other outfits but still we did not do so badly. It was fun to see the bucking horses; there were some every day and it was as good a show as Buffalo Bill's. The men here ride very well; it will be some time before I can tackle a bucking horse. All the horses are rather raw to ride, nothing as good as the English horses. We ride with the cowboy saddles which are very nice and much more comfortable than the English ones. I expect I shall have to get a saddle. I am glad I did not bring out our saddle as no one uses that sort here. They laugh at them.

We have had a good lot of rain during which it was rather bad herding. I was out in the most awful thunderstorm one night. I wanted to get back to camp with the horses as it was 9 o'clock but I could not get them to face the storm. As fast as I turned some of them round, the others would turn their backs to it. I was on top of a hill and the camp was down in the valley and the storm seemed right over my head.

We were close to the mountains and it was very cold most of the time, especially in the morning, but it is very warm now. This place is about 2,000 feet above the sea level, you know, so the mountains do not look so very high, but they do when you get close to them. Distances are very deceiving here. There is a tale of an Englishman who went out to ride to the mountains before breakfast and as he did not come back they went out in the evening to look for him. They found him by a very small stream and on asking him why he did not cross, he said, "Distance is very deceiving here. I thought this might be a river!" They make all sorts of fun of Englishmen here.

Bell's house in town is very small, only 2 little rooms and a kitchen. I have to sleep on the floor in the kitchen on a wagon sheet and a sort of quilt. It is rather hard if you are not used to it but now I sleep like a top. I expect to go out to the ranch in a day or two. I shall have to live under canvas there, as a fellow lives in the house who is on shares with Bell in the ranch. I shall have to get my own bedding, about 3 blankets and a waterproof sheet like the soldiers have.

I think I shall be able to write to you every now and again from the ranch. I will send in a letter at every opportunity. Mind you, keep writing to me all the same as I look forward to any news very much. Please send me something to read and let me know what you send as the Post Office people sometimes steal them. I have no old country news here at all. I will copy out what passes in our local paper for English news: "A friend who called on Mr. Gladstone yesterday afternoon found him deeply engrossed in a game of backgammon." Fancy that rot! It is all the English news in that paper; the rest of it is local politics and scandal.

Bell's boys are very amusing kids. They have just saddled a calf that we have outside to see him buck. One of them is going to ride it for a joke; they can ride anything almost and they are quiet little kids. I have got a wonderful colour now; they hardly knew me here when I came back into town. I think I must make a finish of this letter now as I have to light the fire to roast a piece of beef for dinner as Mr. and Mrs. Bell have driven out to the ranch. This is Sunday. You know, I quite lost count of the days while we were out, as we work Sundays and weekdays just the same.

Mr. Chipman has put what money I did not spend into the savings bank department of the Bank of Montreal. They give me 4%—not bad interest as they are a very safe bank. I think the ranching business pays from what I have heard about it. I have just lit the fire. I wish I had learnt how to cook when I was in London. I hope this meat will be all right. Love to all and tell Father I got the compass all right.

Fort Macleod,
June 29, 1894

Dear Mother,

I came into Macleod yesterday after living by myself at the ranch.[5] I started living in a tent but one day the wind was very rough and blew it down and broke it so I had to shift my quarters into the barn. There is a family living in the house; the man is partners with Bell in the arable land. I have to do all my own cooking. I got on very well considering I could only have a fire between two stones out of doors. I would have rashers of bacon and some dried fruit I boiled up. I also got some mushrooms and sometimes made boiled dumplings out of flour and baking powder. My work was to weed the garden and hoe the potatoes and I enjoyed living there. I had a book lent to me so I was all right till I had finished it. So send me something to read. I thought you were going to send *The Referee* anyhow but it has not arrived. It is all right when I have work to do or something to read but I feel beastly homesick when I have nothing to do. I shall like it better when I have a few friends about here.

My work today has been to clean the harness of Bell's trap. I helped him wash up the plates and dishes and I had to look after the bread baking so I get plenty of variety. We are going up to the other ranch on Monday and shall stop up there for a bit. Mr. Bell and all the children are going up too. I shall get some fishing and after a bit, when the season comes on, plenty of shooting. I wish I had brought out a lot of cartridges with me as they are very dear here. I do not know how long we shall be up at the ranch but I will not be very long as we have another roundup coming on to get some fat cattle to ship.

I think I shall be able to start in this business next year if all goes on well. I shall put my £100 into cattle. They must pay a little; they cost nothing to feed and only the cost of the roundup for looking after them. They are not fed in the winter except the calves and a few weak cows. A good many of the cattle owners do not even do that, but I think the cattle pay for looking after; you do not get so many die. I shall live in the winter at the ranch we are going to now and my work will be to feed Bell's calves. I call it a ranch but it is not one really; it is only a log house on the Government land. The land up there is not surveyed yet so you cannot get any title, though of course when the land is surveyed if you have a place on it, you will be allowed to keep it. Some young Englishmen have just bought a place close to Bell up there. I hope they are nice fellows; it will be nice to have some decent neighbours.

This is a great country for wind. It has been blowing hard. Since writing the above Bell has come in and he and I have got tea for us and the boys. Bell has just gone off with the trap to fetch Mrs. Bell and I have washed all the tea things up. You would have laughed to have seen me up at the ranch having my meals seated on a wagon pole with an upturned stable bucket for a table. I should make a splendid maid of all work now. I forgot to mention I milked the cow this morning and am now looking out for her to come in. It seems funny to you no doubt in a town to let your cow run where it likes but everyone does. The horses are done the same; you simply picket them where there is any grass so it costs nothing to keep a horse. You must understand that there is only one street in this place that can possibly be called a street. The rest of Fort Macleod is simply thrown about anyhow without any reference to street or anything. They are nearly all wooden houses with no upstairs at all to them; some of them are made of logs. The finest buildings in the place are the Police barracks.

Please excuse the writing of this letter as I am standing up writing it on top of the grand piano which nearly fills up the room. The kitchen is hot now as there has been a big fire in the one room. The kitchen is hot now as there has been a big fire in the stove for baking. I also think this is copying ink as it seems to dry like it and it smudges so.

The other side of the river to the ranch on which I have been staying is a Reserve of the Peigan Indians. I watched a lot of them last Sunday shifting their camp. The women had the tent poles tied to their horse with baby on top of the poles, also the tent. I could see them quite plain through my field glasses; it was very amusing. I have spoken to several of the Indians. They always start talking Indian and when they find you do not answer they begin in English. Most of them talk English only they pretend that they cannot. It does not do to say anything before them under the impression that they do not understand you. There are a lot of different tribes about here on their reserves and they come into Fort Macleod very often. Tell Uncle Horace my field glasses are very useful. Everyone has them here. You want them to sort cattle with on the prairie; it saves you a lot of riding if you can see whether it is a band of horses or cows in the distance. I think I shall make a finish of this letter now and go out and post it. I know you are anxious to hear from me. I will write again as soon as I have a chance. I do not expect to get anymore letters from you till I come back from the ranch.

Fort Macleod
Sunday July 8, 1894

My dear Mother,

I shall write this letter to you today but I do not know when I shall have a chance to post it. I have had no letters from you since I wrote last but I expect that there are some for me in Macleod. As I told you in my last letter I am now up at Bell's higher ranch, about 60 miles from Macleod right at the foot of the Mountains. I came up here on Wednesday, at least we started on that day and slept the night in a hut belonging to the Mounted Police. Have I told you that Bell used to be a sergeant in the Police? We got here on Thursday and on Friday Bell left me and is gone back to Macleod. He is coming back this week and is going to bring up Mrs. Bell and the kids to stop a few days. I expect I shall not have a chance to send this letter till they go back to Macleod.

The place up here consists of a log hut just like you see in the pictures; it measures about 5 yards square. It stands in a pretty valley with *trees* and *bushes* in it; there is a large piece of ground fenced in and a cattle corral. My work so far is making a road up the side of a hill so as to be able to come down with the wagon at hay making. It is hard work as the hill is steep and I have a good bit to dig in places. I have a lot of fencing to do when I have done that. This morning I washed my clothes and then darned my socks. I am afraid I have not made such a nice darn as Bab[6] used to do; I thought of her when I did them and saw some of her mending. I picked some pretty lilies, etc. this morning. I wished I could give them to her as she always arranges the flowers at home. There are lots of flowers wild here but they have no smell.

I have a stove in this hut so I get on better with my cooking. I have not made any bread quite by myself yet but I shall have to in a few days. I am boiling some bacon and beans for my dinner tonight. My provisions here are the same as usual. Bell seems to have only one idea of grub. My lot consists of 2 sacks flour, 1 large side bacon, ½ bushel haricot beans, ½ bushel dried apples, tea and a tin of baking powder, 1 sack of sugar, pepper and salt, 1 doz. tins sweet corn, 10 tins tomatoes, matches and candles. Rather large quantities of flour, etc., but that has got to last through haymaking when Bell and a man will be up here as well.

I have got on all right with Bell so far. He is not what you would call a gentleman by any means and is rather rough, but he understands this business and makes money at it. He gives me plenty of work to do. I hope I shall get on all right with him as there is not much work doing here. No one hardly employs anyone as there is not much work to do on a ranch as a rule. Wages are rather low; there are men working at the sawmill for the same wages as I get here. I am sorry to say the Englishmen have not bought the next place up here to Bell's. I wish they had as it is quite close within sight. The people who are in there now are a man and his wife named Read or Reed.[7] I think he is partner with Patterson who owns the ranch. Mrs. Read used to be a servant of Mrs. Bell so they are not much of a companion for me. I have not seen anyone since Friday.

If I am able to start a ranch here, I think I would take up a place around this part as it is a much better part to my eye than down below. There is a lot of grass up here and the cattle all look fat. A man can start well here with about £3,000 capital and can afford to pay 4% for it and pay it off in a few years if he lives carefully. I doubt if Bell has £3,000 in his ranch. Nearly all the men about here are in business in a small way and a funny thing, nearly all have been in the Police. Yet it is quite natural as when a man is in the police round here he sees the country and goes in for ranching as soon as he comes out, and he generally starts with the money he has saved from his pay. There are a few big ranches about who employ several men but not just here.

I have been so busy writing that I forgot about my bacon and the water had nearly all boiled away but I put some more just in time but it stopped boiling sometime in consequence. A good job I am not in a hurry for dinner. I think I shall stop now and fill in some more before the letter goes whenever that is.

It is Sunday again [July 15th] and this letter is not gone yet. I am still by myself and I have seen no one from Macleod for several days. I was quite by myself in the valley as the other people went off to another ranch to start haymaking but they came back yesterday. They could not get on the ground as it was too wet and the flies were very bad. They are getting bad here. It is very lonely here. For several days I only saw a police patrol and an Indian so I am as quiet as I can well be. I wish it was not quite so as I want something to cheer me up.

I did my usual wash this morning and baked some bread. Did I tell you I bought blankets a short time ago for a bed and they charged me $4.60 for a pair of the common grey blankets? They are in one piece and are warm but I never thought they would cost so much. A pair of white leather gloves that one wears here to work costs $2.00. Good pipes are very dear also. I wish I had brought some with me from England. I hope Bell will bring me up several letters and some papers; I have not had any news since I left England. I do not even know what horse won the Derby.

Did I ever tell you that Bell used to have a young fellow working for him last winter? He used to live up here. He was a Canadian from the East. He and Bell had a row and he was sacked; he has joined the Police and is now at Regina doing his drill. I must get Bell to cut my hair, he says he can do it. I had it done by the Macleod barber when I came but I cannot afford his price; he charges 50 cents for cutting it fancy. I think I must leave off again or else this letter will be too big for the post. Bell has just come up and has brought up a fine lot of letters and papers. If Father is so kind as to send me a Daily Tel I should not want the *Weekly Times;* I would sooner have an illustrated paper or one like *Tid Bits* or *Pearson Weekly.*

I have finished my road and the fencing. I hope I am getting on all right here. Bell does not say much to me about work but he never speaks much to me at all. I am working as hard as I know but I cannot do nearly as much as he does and he seems to look at me with a contemptuous sneer as I work. He cannot sack me at a moment's notice out here in the prairie. If he does sack me I hope I shall be able to get another job but it will be hard to get. It would be a pity to leave this part as there is money to be made here in the cattle business before the country gets settled up.

I suppose *The Sketch* would be too expensive a paper to send. Don't bother about it if you think it is.

[No date]

Dear Mother,

Just a few lines to say I am quite well. The ink is dry so I am using pencil. I am in Macleod as I rode in yesterday afternoon. We have a wagon broken down. I found my way all right but I have to go back a different way today as I have to take back some horses from the ranch. I have just got a jolly lot of papers and a letter. Glad to see *The Sketch;* I like that paper. Will write more on Sunday when I get back but do not know when the letter will be posted. I have to take every opportunity sending one. It is so very nasty not being able to write and receive letters regularly. I must make an end of this as I have over 30 miles to go today and it is afternoon now. I am very sorry this is so short. I am scribbling this in the post office where I have found some ink. Bell has not sacked me yet as you can see. I think he is better now.

[No date]

Dear Mother,

As I said in my last letter to you, I was in town when it was written in the Post Office. I was in an awful hurry so now I will tell you all about it. Bell came to me on Thursday as soon as I had done dinner. I had been raking hay all morning. He asked me if I could find my way to town; of course I said I thought I could. Then he told me to saddle up and start at once and try to get a piece for the wagon that was broken and to bring up 2 horses from the other ranch. I put the saddle on and started about ½ past one and I got into Macleod as it was getting dark. Bell had told me to ask for the key of this house and to buy a loaf of bread off the man with the key. When I asked for the bread the chap asked me if I had had supper so I said no and his wife gave me some supper to take over with me. Is it not a silly way to send a fellow on a 60 mile ride, get into town at dark long after the shops are shut and give him no food to take? Breakfast and dinner next day consisted of bread and butter and I left at just about one. I rode 10 miles out to the ranch, got the 2 horses, went as far as a place owned by a Mr. Cockran, and got him to take me in for the night.[8] I got a good supper and breakfast there and reached here at about 5 on Saturday. I had a piece of my loaf left and I ate that for my dinner.

Today (Sunday) Bell came into our hut at 7. (He and Mrs. B sleep in a tent; the other men and I in the hut in a bed.) I was just putting on what few clothes I had taken off to sleep (you know I have slept in my clothes ever since I have been in the country) and was just going to wash when he said, "The first thing you had better do is go and feed those horses you brought up yesterday." I was going on washing when he said, "Go and feed the horses first and wash after." I did not like that much. After breakfast I was watering some horses when Bell came up to me and said, "There is a bit of raking to be finished. I don't care if you do it in the morning or afternoon." I went and did it in the morning so as to try and get the afternoon to write to you and wash my clothes. I don't like having to work Sunday; it always makes me feel miserable when I think of how they used to be spent with you all. This morning when I was raking between 11 and 12 I thought how if I had been at home I should have been in church with you and Bab. You cannot wonder at my wanting to start in business for myself as there is no necessity to live like a pig or to work on Sunday.

I should like to have someone decent to talk to sometimes; it would do me good. Bell hardly ever says anything. I have found out what he was before he joined the Police. He was a plumber and gas fitter.

We are very busy haymaking now; it is work from daylight till dark but I don't mind that. I am feeling very sore generally today after my long ride about 130 miles. I had done no riding since the round up. I think I shall add some more to this letter another day as it cannot go yet.

A week later. Mr. B. is going to take Mrs. B. to town today so I must make a finish of this letter. We have been haying all week; Bell and I have been cutting. It has been very hot all week.

There is a rather good opening for a man to start here now. Our next neighbours are two men, Read and Patterson.[9] Well, Patterson is a queer man to get on with and Read would like to dissolve partnership with him if he can get anyone to buy Patterson out. Patterson wants $6,000 for his half. He has a good lot of cattle and they have 100 steers to sell now which will bring in $4,000. I believe they are included in the price of the ranch. That will be the way I shall make a start, if ever I get the chance, as I would have the benefit of the other fellow's experience.

We are about half way through the hay now. It is a busy season on the prairie with everyone out cutting hay, one against the other, rushing about to cut the best patches. The work has been pretty hard all week from the sunrise to sunset every day, just stopping long enough to eat. I wish I was a bit stronger; I huff and blow like a broken winded cab horse over a job. You know I always was broken winded.

———————————

[No date]

Dear Mother,

I am afraid that there has been a long time between this letter and the one before as I do not know when this will be posted. Bell took my last letter down when he went with Mrs. B. and the kids. He stopped about 2 days and came up here again, then went on a roundup getting beef. He has been gone a fortnight and we expect him back now. He left me and the man to get the hay. We have been at it now for over 5 weeks. I am getting sick of it but it will soon be done now. It is very hard work for only two fellows. I have to fork the hay into my wagon and then drive into the rick and unload both wagons while Larkins[10] makes the rick, then we go out after another load apiece and so on. When Bell was up here he and I brought in the hay while Larkins cut it.

Larkins is not a bad sort of man. He generally works as a cook for some of the big ranches and he earns very good wages at the job, $50 a month. Only he came into town the other day with his money intending to go back to Ireland and went on the bust. He spent it all so Bell got hold of him and got him to come up here haymaking. He abuses Bell's grub very much; it is very poor for men to work hard on. All we have to eat now is potatoes, some green bacon and stewed dried apples. The apples are the best thing but we can hardly eat the bacon. Bell has the name for being very mean with his food and it is quite true. Larkins and I have got on fairly well together although he gets the sulks sometimes (thinking over what a fool he was to bust himself I expect) which is not very lively for me. I have wished myself at home with you all a good many times.

The only time we get a good feed is when I shoot some ducks. I shot some yesterday and we had them for breakfast. I meant to shoot some today but I have had no time yet and I must write to you so as to have a letter ready to post. I expect I shall be able to post it when Bell comes back as he will have to take Larkins back to town as he wants to get another job cooking. We had a nice lot of milk the other day as Mrs. Read went to shop with some people further down while her husband was away and she gave us her cows to milk. Now she has come back again and has her cows back which makes us very sorry for the milk was a great help as we nearly lived on it.

I have been trying to mend my pipe. The only good one I have I brought from England and it got broken the other day. It is an awful pity. I shall write some more before this goes.

Sept. 2, 1894. Larkins is going down to Macleod today and will post this letter for me. Bell has not come up yet so I have had no letter from you for 4 weeks. I wish he had come up as I want to go down to Macleod and get some more clothes. We have had a lot of rain this week and this old roof leaks like anything. The water poured into the hut and wetted everything, including our bed, so we had to sleep in wet things for 2 days before we could dry. We have hardly any food up here and if I could not shoot some ducks and prairie chickens we should be without anything. I must finish as Larkins is going off.

Macleod
(about 60 miles from it really)
Sept 2, 1894

My dear Mother,

I finished my last letter to you this morning but as I have nothing to do just now I will begin this one to you. It is Sunday today and I always feel very homesick on Sunday. It seems so long since I saw you though it is not yet 4 months and I suppose it will be years before I see you again. As I said in my last letter Larkins went to town this morning. Read brought up work from Bell but instead he is going down for another party now. He will be cooking for a roundup party. I hope he will post my letter and not go on a drunk and forget all about it.

I am baking some bread now so I have to keep jumping up to attend to it. My beastly oven won't bake at the bottom so my loaves are done beautifully on top and raw on the bottom. I took them out just now and stood them on top of the stove but that does not answer well. Larkins always did the bread while he was up here. He set it this time but he could not finish it so I had to take it on. It has risen very well but I made one of the loaves too big. I make baking powder bread all right but that is very easy but it is not so good for your health as this yeast bread. My stove is only a common tin thing without any means of heating properly at all. As Larkins often said, we have to rough it out here. I never caught cold from sleeping in the wet bed but it was far from pleasant. The water simply poured on it and whenever I moved a great pool would run inside the bed and I would have to lie in it till my clothes soaked it up. I wish old Bell was experiencing the same. I must leave off now and will write some more later on.

Sunday, Sept. 9th. Another week has gone and Bell has not come up yet. I have not had my letters for over 5 weeks now. It is a shame. I shall be glad when I am on my own account when I shall be able to get my letters at least once a week. I have lived all the week on what I have shot and I have nothing else in the way of meat. I have seen nobody all the week except Read and his wife. I have finished all my papers also so I am pretty lonely.

It has been snowing in the mountains and they are quite white in places. I am glad to say it only rained down here. There have been some prairie fires in the distance. I shall wait again now for a bit and see if Bell comes before I write more.

Sept. 13th, 1894. Bell has just got up here tonight with a large party. They are going up to the mountains fishing and shooting. He is going to take me up with him so I shall have some fun though, of course, I shall have the dirty work to do, cut wood, fetch water, etc. Bell seemed rather repentant when I told him I was out of meat, sugar and lights. He brought me up a jolly lot of letters but left all the books and papers in Macleod as he is going to take me down with him when he goes back.

We had a lot of snow here during the week but it has all melted now, I am glad to say, but it was deep for 2 days. Fancy snow on the 10th of September! Read is gong to Pincher Creek and will post this for me. I will write fuller as soon as I get to Macleod. Set all your minds at rest about me taking a drink. I have not been drinking anything stronger than tea since I have been out here. You cannot get anything else in Macleod.

Macleod,
[No date]

My dear Mother,

I am now down at Bell's other place for a few days and I go back this week to the Kootenay. I have a lot to tell you. I am rather sorry Father sent my letter to Mr. Chipman as he might show it to Mr. Gigot[11] (the Macleod man) who is a friend of Bell's and I spoke rather strongly about him. Of course, Chipman did not know what my work was like as he did not get it but Gigot did for him. Chipman does not know very much about this neighbourhood. He did the best he could for me and was very kind in every way.

I think perhaps it would answer your letters a bit if I told you about the way the cattle business is done here. A man who goes in for cattle in a small way (I am not talking about the company ranches which are different) buys his herd (calves, cows or whatever you like), puts his brand on them with a hot iron and turns them loose. They run just where they like as there are no hedges out here and you can go for hundreds of miles without any. These cattle shift for themselves and to collect them to brand the young calves or to take out the fat steers to sell they have what is called a roundup. Everyone who owns cattle in the district goes out or sends a man and helps collect the cattle. You see, you pay no rent for these cattle and you can have as many as you can buy. Now the winters are very cold and severe here, so it is reckoned a good policy to feed the calves during the winter after they are weaned, also any poor (that is, thin) cows you may have. To enable you to do this, you must have yards or as they are called here, corrals, also a house for you to live in. Now, of course, the best place for you to have this is where you can get plenty of good water and plenty of grass to cut for hay. Now part of the land here can be got under the usual condition but most of it is perfectly free. At present you can go just where you like and build and no one can turn you off until the land is surveyed. Then you must put in your claim for the land, which will be allowed, as the squatter always has the first claim to the land. So you understand a rancher's business is to build his corrals and put up his hay and feed his calves in winter. Now to save expense in putting up hay and living, etc., men will often go into partnership. Each man keeps his own cattle which he can always know by his brand but they work together in cutting up the hay and are together for company. That is what I meant by going in with a man.

I would like to buy some cattle in the spring and either take up a place and build myself or buy a place ready built, if I saw one I should like and everything suited. But of course before next spring things may alter. Something may turn up, so it is rather early yet to say anything definite. It is a satisfaction to know that I could have some money if an opening offered that would be worth taking, say someone selling their cattle or place. Of course, in starting you want to buy your cattle of all ages; if you only bought cows or calves you might have to wait 3 or 4 years before you had anything to sell, even though your herd would be increasing in numbers every year. Anything more you want to know please ask.

I must now tell you about my doings. As I said in my last letter, Bell came up to the Kootenay with a large party to go fishing and shooting. We went on the next day to the Kootenay [Waterton] Lakes and camped there, right at the very foot of the mountains. I was very glad to get right up to them; I have so often wanted to do so. We only stopped there one night as game was scarce and the food ran out. Old Watson,[12] the man who rents Bell's stable land on this ranch, got lost and we did not find him until 11 o'clock at night. Bell, Davis and I went out firing guns and shouting till we found him. There is a lot of bush up there and he got lost in that. He must be rather a duffer though to get lost in such a place.

The next day we came back halfway to the ranch, then the ranch, then Macleod. We got more game round the ranch than we did anywhere else. We came from the ranch to Macleod in one day. I came out to the ranch on the Belly river instead of going to Macleod and went into Macleod with a load of hay to Bell's house the next day.

They have been having a small show and some races in Macleod 3 days last. I saw them on Thursday the last day; I wish I could have shown them to you for you would then see the Wild West. Going out to the race ground was a sight to see. You would think it was Buffalo Bill's turned loose. There were cowboys in their get-up, Indians in blankets and red paint, and people driving in buggies, sulkies, wagons, and buckboards all going as hard as they could. Then there were the races. There was a trotting match but that was nothing; you can see that anywhere. Then came a cowboy race which my friend Reed won easily. In a cowboy race you ride up course, round a barrel, back around another one, and home. Of course you must ride a good cow horse to turn so short. Then there was riding the bucking horses for a prize. It was very good; they got all the worst horses they could and they did buck. One man got thrown, or as they say here, fired.

Then we had an Indian race. It was very amusing from the start. The Indians were all drawn up in line waiting when one of the cowbys came right in amongst them with a bucking horse. You should have seen them go! It started the race all right; they went for their lives with the cowboy after them. The bucking horses come right into the crowd sometimes. I got a safe position on top of a fence while that was going on. Then we had roping the wild steer. They had several steers in a corral. The boy who is going to rope is on his horse waiting outside. They let out one steer and when it is clear of the crowd and running away, they sing out "go!" The cowboy takes after it, catches it round the head with his lariat, throws it down and ties its legs together so it cannot get up. The man who ties his quickest wins. They take the time from when they say go. A lot depends on your horse as while you are tying the steer's legs, the horse has to keep the rope tight and hold the steer down. Reed also won this; his time was 2 min. 12 sec. The next man was 2 min. 17 sec. Very close was not it? Pretty quick work too when you think what a lot there is to do single handed. There were a lot of other races as well but these were the best.

I am now for a few days helping Old Watson get in a little hay and dig his potatoes. When he has done with me I go back to the Kootenay. Bell is away on a roundup branding calves.

Do you think you could find me a warm woolen comforter to go round my neck, also cuffs for my wrists? They do not make very good ones here, I am told, so they nearly all use shawls but a comforter is better. I am going to buy my over-shoes, cap, and a pair of blankets this week. My next letter will be from the Kootenay but when it will be posted I do not know. I am going to make some more corrals up there so shall have a lot of poles to cut in the brush and holes to dig.

[No date]

My dear Mother,

I am afraid it is again a long time between this letter and the last. I have not heard from you since your birthday. I am up at the Kootenay still. I am feeding the calves and jobbing around generally. I mudded up the spaces between the logs in the stable, also the same to my hut. I shall have a job to fill out my letters now as there will be no variety in my work and I shall see nobody or nothing. I went down to the calf roundup on Saturday; they were about 4 miles off. I went with Reed and a man called Shorty. I got 5 cows and calves of Bell's. Shorty had been on the roundup and had brought in what calves of ours he had found. He is still away on the roundup. I expect him back in a day or two when I shall wean all the calves he brings me. He works for Morgan & Cummins;[13] they have a ranch about 3 miles down the creek below Reed and Patterson. They do not live there but keep 2 men at the ranch.

The weather has been fine and mild lately owing to our having a west wind. It varies in temperature very much, though some mornings the creek is nearly frozen over (and it flows swift too). Other days you go about in shirt sleeves. I hope it will keep warm as long as it can as it saves my firewood. It is an awful nuisance getting wood; most people burn coal but of course they would not give it to a hired man.

I have treated myself to some butter; it is very good. You have no idea how you like it when you have not had any for months. The same with milk. It must seem funny to you, me working in a cow camp and not having any milk. I had a meal with Patterson the other day and he used *condensed* milk in his tea and he has ½ share in 500 head of cattle. I must stop now for a bit and try and find some more news.

Since writing the above we have had some awful weather. We had snow and frost and an east wind. The temperature was below zero. The creek that goes by this place was frozen right across, strong enough to bear up a man and horse and it is a swift mountain stream too. I do not know the exact degree it went to as I left my little thermometer at home when I came away. We had a chinook two days ago, I am glad to say, and it nearly melted all the snow, but it is freezing hard again now. The changes in two hours are tremendous; it all depends on the wind. It is always blowing hard from somewhere.

We have to dress up when it is cold. I wear a cap that comes over my ears, a pair of overalls as well as trousers, German socks instead of boots, and rubber overshoes that come as high as an ordinary boot, and mitts on my hands. Mitts are very thick woolen gloves with all the fingers in one. The cold is much worse than I ever felt in England and we have not had anything yet the people say about here. I never saw running water freeze like that. Of course, I have never had it to zero before. All the papers I get, like *Pearsons* and the *Sketch Today*, etc., are eagerly taken by the others around here when I have done with them and they get passed on all over the country. The wolves killed 3 calves of Morgan & Cummins yesterday. I hope they don't get at mine. Must finish at once as Patterson is going to Macleod and will post this. He is waiting now.

[No date]

My dear Mother,

I am up at the Kootenay again, as I expect you have guessed by the length of time between this letter and my last. I have been to church today. A parson from Pincher Creek came up to one of the rancher's houses and had a service and sacrament. I am sorry to say he will not be out again till the spring unless the weather keeps very open. The rancher's name is Berry.[14] They have a very nice little house and the room we were in was well furnished and looked like an English drawing room. Mrs. Berry is English. We had a heavy fall of snow last week, it was very deep but it is nearly all gone now. I am busy putting up a fresh corral for the calves and I also have to ride the range every day as we have most of the cows and calves up here. We want to keep them here till we wean them. I had rather a better time while working for Watson as he has 3 daughters who do the cooking. They got up a dance one night with some men from the next ranch and at other times someone often came over in the evening. I suppose you have heard from Mr. Chipman. I saw Mr. Gigot when I was in Macleod and he told me that Mr. Chipman had spoken to him about me, saying he had heard from us. He told me to try and make the best of it, etc., etc. He agreed that I ought not to have been left without meat but no doubt it could not have been helped. I do not think he liked any grumbling about Bell, as he is a friend of his.

I have a cat here now who is much interested in this letter but I could not consider a dog. I have not done any shooting lately, being too busy. I shot a goose when I was at the other ranch. I thank you all very much for the letters and papers.

[Later]. Another Sunday and I still have this letter; Bell has not come up so I have not heard from you for a long time. My birthday passed very quietly. The only person I spoke to was an Indian who was out after wolves. He was a very decent sort of chap and so were his companions; they belong to the Stoney Tribe so I suppose that tribe is better than some of the others. They killed a wolf about a mile from here. I often hear the wolves howling at night. I wish I could kill one as you get $5 for its scalp from the Government. I have plenty of beef now as Bell left me nearly a ¼ of beef which is hanging up outside. It shows how cold it is, as it keeps quite fresh. I have been cutting poles when I am not riding around the stock, which takes me about 2 or 3 hours every morning. My kitten kills mice beautifully but it tortures them for about an hour so I call her Linger Tiger

Lucy; my first name was Daisy Bell but I thought Bell might think it personal.

[October 5, 1894]

My dear Mother,

Bell has just got up and I have a chance to send this letter down by him so I must hurry and finish it.

Thank Father very much for the pipes. I have not got them yet as Bell could not get them till I had paid the $1.40 duty. I do not know if the duty is high because they came through the States. On the advice card they say "Parcel from the United States."

I am still with Bell as you see. I do not know how I can leave him this winter as if I do my chances of getting another job are very small as there is nothing doing in the winter in this country. The cold is so intense that work out of doors (except feeding cattle) is impossible and as that only requires a few men, one is lucky to get a job. I cannot afford to do nothing so I think I had better stop where I am and put up with the discomforts. In the spring I will try to buy some cattle and put up a little place, that is, of course, if I can get the capital to do it with.

I have had a hard day's work today, hauling the poles I have cut from the woods to the yard. As you see, I have some fresh beef now and shall have it all through the winter as it gets frozen hard and keeps well. I think I have nothing more to say just now.

Kootenay,
December 6, 1894

My dear Father,

I have just received your 3 letters which were brought up to me with the rest of my mail by a neighbouring rancher. I have considered the matter of a farm in England and I think it would be very foolish of me to go home now as things are at present. You see, with £1,000 I should only be able to take a very small farm and I should not be able to better myself. But here I shall if not unlucky be able to double my money in a few years. Of course, I may have bad seasons or my cattle may get ill which would throw me back, but the same could happen on a farm in England. The life of a large farmer, like those I used to live with in England would be far nicer than living out here, but I doubt if a small farmer is much better. I know that life here is very rough, especially for me now as they do not trouble much about the comfort of a hired man. This hut, for instance, if it belonged to me, could be made better for a very few dollars. It is only 9 feet square so sufficient boards to make a floor would not cost much. Also, the difference in price between a good cooking stove and this sheet iron one is not much and the comfort is a great deal. I shall also get myself better food when on my own account. I shall not do anything till the spring and not without consulting Mr. Chipman. My first idea is to build a ranch in the spring and buy cattle as I see the chance. Of course, I shall have to keep some money to live on, as I shall not have any coming in for 3 years unless I can buy some older cattle, but they are not often sold.

Do you remember my speaking about a Percy Kenard (a doctor's son) in my first letter? He is stopping with Patterson now for the winter. If I build a ranch he will very likely help me and live with me, sharing expenses. It would be cheaper for both of us, besides it is bad to be quite alone as if you get ill or hurt you might die before anyone found it out. We should not be partners in any way; it is only like two men sharing a room in London. It would save both of us having to hire labour in haymaking. He is a nice chap and steady so I hope we may manage it. But, of course, I will write to Chipman first.

I hope Mother will not be disappointed at my wanting to stop out here. When I do start in England I should come nearer to London than Dorset. As far as climate goes England is far ahead of this country.

[No date]

My dear Mother,

I got the box all right and am awfully pleased with the contents. The gloves are splendid though, of course, not thick enough when it is very cold but they do well when it is moderate. I enjoyed the cake very much; none of it was eaten on the road not even the piece in the paper. I am still at Kootenay and shall be so. The calves are doing very well and they are all very tame. I have named them after celebrated people, principally theatrical.

You remember my writing about Percy Kenard (the doctor's son) who is stopping with Patterson now for the winter? I am glad he is there as he makes a good companion for me. I go and see him and vice versa. I hope he will help me with my ranch in the spring. He is busy trying to poison wolves and coyotes now. He has killed some coyotes and a dog or two, but no wolves yet. The owners of the dogs are indignant.

It is very cold but when the wind does not blow it is not bad. We have had a fine time lately with no snow. Bell is up here now for a few days; he is going to kill a cow so I shall get fresh beef again. It is not bad here as I have not much to do but feed the cattle. I have to ride about them nearly every day for 4 or 5 hours.

I have had an invitation from Mr. Gigot to spend Christmas with him so I shall go down to Macleod for a few days. It is very kind of him to ask me as I was not looking forward to Xmas. I hope you are not sorry I want to stop out here. I think when I am on my own account I shall like it better. I know the business pays better. When I get things in good working order I shall be able to come over and see you; the journey is not long and I shall be able to do it cheap.

We have just killed a cow and she is very good meat. I went out shooting with Bell this afternoon; we did not kill much as the birds are so wild. Things have been going on pretty well lately so I am in pretty good tune.

[No date]

My dear Mother,

I am up by myself again as Bell has gone down. I sent my last letter to you down by him. I am glad to say that we are going to have the mail come to a place about 5 miles from here so I shall be able to get my letters regularly as they will be sent on from Macleod. I am glad to say the weather is still fine. I hope it will keep fine till Xmas as if it storms I shall not be able to do down. I do not want to get caught in a blizzard and frozen to death nor yet lose my way. I shall take 2 days over the ride down as the days are short and my pony is only fed on hay. I let the calves out of the corral into the pasture during day now; they are quite weaned and it does them good to get a little exercise. I have to keep an eye on them all day as they can easily get out into the prairie as the fence is only made of 2 strands of barb wire and they can get under it.

I am getting my supper now and have just made my tea. I do not have a tea pot but put the tea into the kettle I boil the water in, the same with coffee. I have not shot much lately as I have plenty of beef and go in for cold roast beef or fry some. There were some Indians round the other day, they had shot several deer. I should like to see some deer so I must try and go right up into the mountains.

I am busy decorating my hut with pictures from the *Sketch* and *St. Pauls'*. I like *St. Pauls'* as it has more pictures even than the *Sketch*, I think. I expect if you were out here now you would go skating. There is no trouble about the ice not bearing out here. It would bear a railroad and it never thaws at least not at the spring. If I go to Macleod I shall post this letter myself so I shall leave the rest to fill in down there.

December 24, 1894

Dear Mother,

I am down in Macleod. I came down in a day as the weather was fine. I found a lot of letters for me including a long one from McGee written before he was ill. I wish when you see him you would thank him for it. Also please thank Aunt Emily for her presents; I am going to get it out of customs now. I have had a jolly lot of papers from you all but I have not had your card yet.

I must finish as I have a lot to do before I go to Mr. Gigot's. I shall be very pleased to see Father if he comes out and will get him to bring some things so as to get them duty free. More soon from me.

Kootenay,
January 3, 1895

My dear Sister,

I wish you very much happy returns of the day. I wish I could give it in person but you may be sure I am thinking about you today and will have a birthday feast. My cat, calves and horses will have an extra feed. I suppose you will have a lot of presents. I wish I could have got you something out here. A few Indian scalps would have made a very nice trimming for your dress and quite unique, only there have been no Indians to kill around here lately. Some bear claws would have made a necklace worthy of the sister of a frontiersman, only the bears have also kept out of the way so I have asked Mother to invest my small donation for me. I hope you will still continue to send me your charming letters which I enjoy more than any I get.

> Believe me, your affc. brother,
> Long haired Claude,
> the Lone Cowboy of the
> Rockies, alias C.W.E. Gardiner.

Kootenay,
January 10, 1895

Dear Mother,

I am back at work again after a jolly time at Macleod. I went down on Sunday as I told you in my last letter and on Monday I went up to Mr. Gigot's. Mr. Gigot has just finished having his house done up and it was not yet straight so I did not sleep there but in the store with Mr. Hunter, the bookkeeper to the H.B. Co.[15] I had dinner with Gigot and his wife on Monday and on Tuesday (Xmas day) I went to Church in the morning. Afterwards, Hunter and I went to lunch with Mr. Campbell, the postmaster.[16] Hunter and I then went to Gigots for our Christmas dinner and we stopped there till 9 p.m. Afterwards, Hunter & I went up to the barracks to Captain Casey's house.[17] I was introduced to him the day before and he had asked Hunter & I to look in during the evening; he asked us to dinner but of course I could not go. I could have got plenty of Xmas dinners as I was asked to the G troop mess dinner as well. I was introduced to a good many of the police officers while I was down.

I spent Wednesday with the Gigots and on Thursday I came away the first thing in the morning. The Gigots are a nice family. They are German but the children are more English; they cannot speak a word of German. There are 7 children, 3 boys and 4 girls. The eldest is a boy about 17, he is a clerk in the bank at Macleod. The next 2 are girls, jolly little girls, then I don't know how they run but the youngest is a girl. Gigot has a nice house beautifully furnished and carpeted; he gave a very good dinner. I don't think I had such a bad time after all, do you?

Gigot had a talk about things with me. He knows of a man and has written to Chipman about him who he (Gigot) thinks would be a good man for me to go in with. Chipman is going to see this man, who is now down East. I don't know if anything will come of it. This man (Stewart is his name) used to have a ranch and cattle in the Porcupine Hills. He sold out last year to his late partner but he wants to buy the place and cattle back again. Stewart has some capital but not enough to pay that chap out. I don't know if I shall hear anything about it from Chipman and I don't know what sort of man Stewart is to get on with. I know he is a very good cowboy and a good sort of chap for his kind, but I don't quite like the idea of being partners with one of those fellows. You see, it is a job to divide up again if you don't get on together.

Reed and Patterson are a warning against partners; they want to divide up badly. Pat told me that they will divide the cattle on the spring roundup. If I went in by myself, I think I could not do better than buy their ranch. They must sell it. It consists of one frame house in 2 rooms which cost $300; a log hut which Pat lives in which has a boxed roof and floor; a pine log stable where each log cost them 40 cents; some good yards and another shed or two. There are two good springs on the place that never freeze and it is in a very good position. I can buy it for $500, perhaps less, but I don't think it would be dear. If I bought it, I should put up hay with Bell and we would wean our calves together. I think this is a good idea. I like this part and I think if I put up a place myself it would cost me as much as that, even if I could find such a good situation.

I am sorry to say that the post will not run up here till April. Do you remember my buying a pair of leather braces at Hopes? They told me I could get duplicate buckle ends so I wish you would see if they have them still. The braces were *all* leather.

Everyone told me how much better I was looking than when I came out. I have got much broader and can hardly button my waistcoats. We had the temperature at 28° below zero a day or two ago and I think yesterday was even colder. We are having a very cold spell just now with snow up to one's knees. They were skating on the river at Macleod. I shall be glad when it thaws a bit; fancy it has been freezing since October though the weather has been beautiful till now.

P.S. If I go in with Stewart, I don't know how much money it will take but if I go by myself I could do with £800. I should have some in the bank so as I draw it as required so I could buy anything cheap. You can do this if you can lay your hands on the cash at once. 40 head of stock were sold the other day at a little over $10 a head by a man who wanted to get away at once. They were the cheapest lot sold in Macleod for a long time. I wish I had had the cash as it was a good snap. You can often pick up small lots cheap if you have the cash. These fellows want money and have to sell out to get it.

Kootenay,
Jan. 21, 1895,

My dear Mother,

I have just got a letter from Grandfather in which he says "you may doubtless have heard of the crime I have committed." He also says it cannot be considered a wise act but he was left along and could not bear his loneliness any longer. He could not persuade Ada's mother to let her come as housekeeper so was compelled to ask her to marry him. His punishment is very severe in that you won't dine with him. He ought to look on it in the light of another dinner saved. He says also it will not take from his children or grandchildren one shilling of any property he may have to leave.

I was very sorry to see in your letter of the death of Mr. McGee. I told you that I had a letter from him at Christmas. To think that when I got the letter the poor chap was dead. I always admired him very much, he was a thorough man as well as a person. There was no humbug about him. I am sure all the boys and young men of the parish will miss him as much as anyone.

Patterson has been back into Pincher Creek and has

brought out my letters but no papers as he was on horseback. I have had my letters sent to the Creek with the idea of coming up here but, as I told you before, the post does not run till April. I was much amused in your letter where you tell me you now date your letters outside and I never date mine at all. I forget to date mine sometimes as I always date it the last thing as I never know when it will be posted.

In Father's letter he talks about bringing out a camp bed. I don't think I shall want one as I shall get a proper bedstead when I start a ranch. I should like him to bring me some blankets, about 2 pair. I shall also want 2 pair of moleskin or corduroy trousers but I will tell him about that when the time is close. I shall want him to bring me out a lot of cartridges as they cost here, loaded $4.50 (18s.) and load myself $3.50 (14s.) At the A&N they cost about 9s. Of course, there will be the extra carriage and duty on them. I want Father to bring a *good* deck chair; they are very comfortable to sit in and make handy furniture. I can get thermometers pretty cheap in Macleod.

I will ease your minds again by saying my health has never been better. I do not find the cold knocks me up at all. Of course, I wrap up for it. I *always* wear 2 pair of trousers. When I ride and it is a cold day I put on 2 pair of the German socks, a pair of rubber overshoes, 2 overcoats, cap over my ears, woolen comforter, and a pair of woolen mitts with a pair of buckskin ones over them. You can only see my eyes. The worst is the weather changes; today it is comparatively mild as there is a west wind but yesterday was about 20° below zero. The wind will melt the snow but it is not enough to thaw the ice or the ground. The ice on the creek must be nearly 2 feet thick and I can ride across it on horseback anywhere. It is a nuisance keeping a hole open for the cattle to drink. Everyone says we are having a wonderful winter; certainly we have had very few storms. The cattle are all fat which saves me a lot of work feeding.

My time with Bell will soon be up. I expect he will want me to go about the end of April, if not before; it depends when we have done feeding. Anyhow I shall want to be working for myself then. I have not heard from Gigot since I came up so I do not know if he has heard or done anythng more about Mr. Stewart.

My kitten is getting a fine cat. You would never think it was the half starved little brute that I had at first. It belonged to the daughter of a rancher on this creek who left their ranch and the cat too. Reed found it nearly dead. It is most intelligent, sits on my shoulder and sleeps in my bed. What made you think we could not drive a wagon up here? You can drive anywhere on the prairies; there is not a hedge or a bush or a tree and hardly a hill betweeen here and Macleod. Anything more monotonous you never saw.

Kootenay,
February 8, 1895,

My dear Mother,
We have had it very cold lately. The night before last the temperature was 38° below zero and continued so nearly all yesterday, but today is warmer. Nearly all the water in my hut froze solid even though I had a fire going. It is cold work riding; you have to cover up well to prevent getting frozen. The wolves have been giving a concert all day. I hope they have not killed anything. They have a very melancholy cry , like a human being howling, but the coyote makes a cheerful bark like a little terrier.

I have been having my mail sent to Pincher Creek so I have been getting it oftener. Berry brought it up this last time and took a lot down to post for me. Kennard is still stopping with Patterson so I often see him. Patterson has given me a photo they had taken of the fall roundup so I will send it to you one day when I get the chance. Nearly all the men I have spoken to you about are in it and it gives you an idea of the prairie. I am expecting Bell up every day now. I expect he will come the first day the weather is good. The work goes on the same as usual; one day is exactly like another. In fact you hardly ever know what day of the week it is and as for the time, nobody knows that with any certainty. You know when it is dark at night and you have to light up. Then after you have worked or read enough you go to bed. I have to do my washing tonight so I shall not write much more as the water is nearly hot. I wish I could get someone to do it for me as I hate the job. Patterson gets his done at the Creek and so should I if I was my own master and could take it down. You should see the darns I put in my socks.

Read, Kennard, another chap and myself rode up to the mountains yesterday rode up to the mountains yesterday to go through all the cattle that were up in the bush. I had never been so far up before. The country is very pretty, all lakes and thickly wooded; it is difficult to ride through as the bush is so thick. It must look pretty in the summer when they are all green but of course now everything is covered with snow. It has been very fine today, a perfectly blue sky. I thought how we should enjoy a day like this in old England with everyone out skating. Nobody skates up here, though they do in Macleod. I am going to take this letter down to Berrys on the chance that he is going into the Creek soon.

Kootenay,
March 4, 1895,

My dear Father,

I have just got your letter telling me about Grandfather giving me a £1000 for a start. I am very glad to get it. In my last letter home I said that any money for me could come through the H.B. Co. I am going to see Gigot and talk the matter over with him before I do anything about a ranch. I expect to be up here till on in April but it depends a good bit on the weather as to when we leave off feeding. Of course, I shall not quit Bell till that is done. Bell has been up here the last few days riding with me getting in cattle. I have got about 100 head to feed now. We have had a good bit of snow the last week but it is melting a bit now. I wish a Chinook would get up and blow it away; it is so bad to ride in as you keep getting into deep drifts. I am just about out of ink; it is an awful job to write. I must rustle some more from somewhere.

I don't think much of your six shooter. I blazed away at a skunk with it the other night; I hit it once but did not kill it and it got away. I could smell it for days. The other night some wolves came down to the shack. I jumped out of bed and took the six shooter and ran out but it was very dark and I could not see them although I heard them run away in the grass. The boys out here use the Colt frontier pistols, those with a long barrel and .44 cal; they are much better to shoot with. They carry them to kill wolves.

Mother asks what thermometer we use out here. Zero is 32° below freezing and the coldest we have had is 38° below zero. Some winters they get it colder than that. Bell and I have made a sledge for me to pull the hay as I have so many cows to feed. I hitch up one of the horses and just go sailing; it saves a lot of carrying. Bell is pleased with his cattle.

Kootenay,
April 4, 1895,

My dear Mother,

I have just got your first letter written from Rome. It is not necessary to still put J. Bell on my letters as I am well known now and most likely by the time you answer this I shall not be with him. I went into Pincher Creek last Tuesday, the first time I have been anywhere since Xmas. I wanted to get a pair of overalls and a neck handkerchief, also some ink and paper. I hoped I should have found some letters telling me my money was in Macleod but there were no letters for me at all. I had a 40 mile ride for nothing, as it were, as I went in that day especially to meet the post. I got a nice lot of papers though. I rode in in 3 hours exactly and the same coming out—not a bad journey in a day for my little pony. The snow is melting fast now; there is only a little left in the side of the hills. The grass is beginning to show too, so I hope that we are done with the winter. I have 4 young calves round here now of Bell's. I expect to turn them all out in a day or two. As soon as Bell comes up, we shall close this place and I shall go down to Macleod. I had a shot at a goose just now but I did not kill it. They take a lot of hitting with a shotgun to stop them; a rifle is best only I cannot get cartridges for mine.

Pincher Creek is a very small place and very quiet the day I was in. I think I was the only visitor in the place. I did not see anyone else. The post is going to start coming up to this creek next week but it will not make much difference to me as I shall be going down. Give my love to all.

P.S. I shall have to ride about 4 miles each way to the post office to get my letters when the post comes up to this creek. They never deliver letters in America. I have not been able to get this letter off yet but I am going to post it as the mail is going to run from this creek tomorrow. Bell has not come up yet but I am expecting him every day. I wish he could hurry up as I want to see Gigot and make some arrangements about starting for myself. The spring has come so one wants to begin now if one is going to do anything this year, as the season is short.

—————————

Macleod,
April 28, 1895,

My dear Mother,

I am down in Macleod now and have just got your letters. I am very sorry to hear that Father is not coming out here this year as I had been looking forward to see him. But perhaps he may be able to come out next year.

I am very busy now and have been for the last week or two. I am working with Mr. Bell out at his ranch on the Belly River where I have been ploughing all the week. It is not at all bad fun as I have a sulky plough (one of those you ride on) and I drive up and down all day.

I am thinking of buying a half share in Bell's cattle. No doubt you will be surprised to hear this, after I could not get on with him at first. But since last October we have got on very well together and everyone advises me to do so. Mr. Bell is a very straight man and would deal fairly with a man. I should not, of course, live with him but should live up at the place on the Kootenay. He is going to build a frame house up there for me so I shall run my own place entirely. I am paying $20 a head for the cattle, which is a fair price. He reckons to have about 400 head or more but it is impossible to get a count on them without branding them all over again as you often miss quite a few on the roundups. He says I can take the opinion of any of the cowmen on the subject if I am not satisfied with the numbers. I also have his brand book to refer to which gives the number branded every year. There will be $1,000 worth of steers to sell this year in which I shall share so I begin to get an income from the cattle at once and that will increase every year. We are expecting to brand over 100 calves this year and the steers will very likely fetch more money than that as cattle seems to be going up in price. He will find 10 horses for the outfit in which I will have a half share—wagons, mowers, rakes, harness, etc. I will also have a half share in the Belly River ranch in that I would take a half share in all the crops that we raise there though, of course, I would not have a share in the ownership of that place. He would want quite a bit for that as he has the deeds

Claude Gardiner, owner of the Wineglass Ranch, west of Fort Macleod.

Claude Gardiner's first dwelling on the Wineglass Ranch, winter of 1907-08.

Claude Gardiner, arriving in Fort Macleod after a fifteen-mile ride from his ranch in February, 1910.

Claude Gardiner, relaxing in his sitting room at the ranch, January 1910.

View of the Wineglass Ranch about 1896.

Claude Gardiner, February 8, 1906.

Longhorn cattle drifting through Claude Gardiner's ranch.

Blood Indians gathered for races near Dr. O.C. Edwards's house during a visit by the Gardiners.

Cattle on the Wineglass Ranch.

View of the Wineglass ranchhouse in October 1907.

Claude Gardiner, English ranchman, c. 1907.

Coyote hunt on the 44 Ranch west of Nanton, February 1906. Left to right: Messrs. Henson, Clarke and Latham, Alice Edwards, and Claude Gardiner. Alice and Claude were married a year later.

The wedding of Claude Gardiner and Alice Edwards in 1907. Left to right: "Bab," Mr. Peard, Alice Edwards, Claude Gardiner, Miss Macdonald, and Mr. Nichol.

Claude Gardiner (extreme right), his new wife Alice (extreme left) with friends at the Wineglass Ranch, c. 1907.

for the place which is over 1,000 acres. I think it is a fair arrangment and I like the idea of it.

Bell likes the idea as he thinks he can make more % out of a half share in his cattle than he does now when he has wages to pay, etc. A man by himself is very much handicapped in working his cattle as they range over such an extent of country. In the way we are going to work it, I shall ride that country up there and Bell down here. I think we are likely to get on as we shall not be living in the same place together which is where some fellows fall out. When you see the same chap day after day and all day you are bound to have a row sooner or later. Bell is a man who has made all his money out of cattle, or nearly all, so is more likely to get on than a man who had made a failure of them. Of course, I know more about the cattle too, all those I have been feeding in the winter, etc., and they are a very good class of cattle. There are no better on the range.

If I was by myself, I should have to hire a man for the first few roundups or I should very likely get done out of some of my cattle. It is not the easiest job in the world to cut out your cattle from a bunch of several head. I think I told you that our brand is ⌒ on the left ribs and on the shoulder for horses. It is called the half circle bar ranch. Mr. Gigot thinks I cannot do better than go in to this outfit.

With regards to Father's six shooter, I use the English cartridges that I brought with me. They fit it quite well but you cannot make very good shooting with a short barrelled gun. An English Army revolver is no good here either as you cannot get English cartridges. The .45 (by mistake I wrote .44) is the only size the boys carry and they are all Colt's frontier pattern in a scabbard with a belt stuck full of cartridge. As Father is not coming out it does not matter now.

Macleod,
May 12, 1895,

My dear Mother,

The last fortnight I have been a farmer's boy, ploughing nearly every day. We have put in quite a lot of potatoes and are putting in a lot of oats for hay which we shall cut green. I have not gone in with Bell yet but I am expecting to see Gigot today to hear his opinion on some of the prices of different things. I have left him a memo to look over to see if he thinks they are all right.

I was out riding all day yesterday with Franklin[18] and a crowd helping him gather his mares. We started before 8 and did not get back till ½ after 6, riding fast nearly all the time. As a consequence I am tired and sore today. I have not been riding hard for a little time now and it soon plays one out if you are not always at it. We rounded up about 200 horses. Franklin gave me a very good horse to ride and we had good fun. They are out riding today after some more horses but I rode into here this morning.

I have been to church like a good boy. We are having fun in our church now; the parson is high church and they take up the collection just as the people are sitting down. Then they take the money up to the parson who stands in front of the altar and holds it over his head. The harmonium plays and we have to stand up and sing something or other; no one knows what it is except the choir. We think it is Latin but are not certain. This performance is new and we don't like it, so a good many won't stand up when he does it, and hence the row. He preached at us finely this morning but it had no effect.

They are going to have a calico ball in this place next week and we have got up a good joke if it comes off. One of the boys is a great ladies man and dresses up finely so when the calico business was started, we told him that all the men had to go in pyjamas. We made up a fine yarn as to what we were going to wear and he has gone and ordered a suit. If he goes to the ball in it I shall go to see him. It will be a joke to see him walk in. I am afraid that he may get to hear that it is a plant and come in ordinary dress like the others, but it has gone all right so far. I shall hear if he is going in pyjamas on the day. I shall not go if he does not as it is no fun dancing after you have been working hard.

I am sending a power of attorney by this post but I don't know if it will do for Father to get the money for me. If not, he had better send me one of the usual forms that they use in England when you want anyone to draw money for you.

———————

Macleod,
May 26, 1895

My dear Mother,

I have done nothing more about Bell yet. I am waiting to hear from Winnipeg. I wish they would hurry up as the round-up starts on Thursday week and it all has to be settled by then. I think Gigot might have been a bit quicker over it as he knows that one cannot make arrangements to go out to roundup in a day. One has to make arrangements about messing, saddle horses, etc. All last week I have been ploughing and we have nearly done now. The week before, I was on the horse roundup with Bell getting all our mares and colts. We had fine weather but it was very dusty separating the horses as you may imagine; 500 horses in a small yard can make quite a dust. I saw some fine bucking. Franklin had a horse he was riding that is a regular outlaw. He bucked for a long time when he was mounted first and every time he was galloped he would start in again but Franklin has nearly cured him of it now. He is a good rider. They reckon him the best in the Territory.

We are wanting rain badly here now as we have had none since September. The snow does not count for much as it all blows off into the valleys and the ground is frozen hard when it falls.

I did not go to the Ball as I was too busy on the roundup to get away. That fellow did not wear his pyjamas as some duffer started telling him how his coat was being trimmed for the dance and he went and had his done the same. The men all had their coats done in fancy colours; it must have looked very amusing. Things are very quiet here now; nothing going on till roundup. It is going to be a big affair this year. The weather is still cold when the sun goes in and the nights are cold. On the horse roundup we had to tent so it was pretty cold but it did not rain so we were all right.

I was sorry to hear that Grandfather has been ill but hope he is better now. I must finish this letter now as I am out of news.

———————

Macleod,
June 6, 1895,

My dear Mother,

The business with Bell is all off. I heard from Winnipeg and they confirmed Mr. Gigot's advice which was not to go in unless Bell agreed to have a count on the cattle and this he would not do. Bell says it knocks the cattle about to brand them over again. You have to do this when you count them or you cannot tell afterwards what cattle have been counted as you do not always get everyone the first time of rounding them up. I think Bell was afraid he had not got the number of cattle he claims or he would not have objected to have a count on them. I wish Mr. Gigot had given me his opinion sooner in the deal so I should not have wasted so much time.

I left Bell yesterday and have taken a room in town while looking about. I can live very cheaply in town in a nice clean place, a Temperance Hotel they call it. You bet I slept last night. I have not slept in such a bed for a long time. I was glad to leave Bell's house in town; it is small and full of children and I had to sleep on the kitchen floor.

I have been to look at a ranch in the Porcupine Hills that is for sale. The H.B. Co. have a mortage on it and they are going to sell it. They have the deeds of the place so that one cannot be turned off it by anyone. It is very good land and grows a good crop so that one has something to help besides the cattle. Of course, I could homestead next to it and so get a good sized ranch. The place as it stands now is 160 acres or a ¼ section. There is a house of several rooms, stables, corrals, etc. There is also a good spring which runs winter and summer and does not freeze up. I shall not decide about this place for a week or two so as to see if anything else turns up that is any good.

Tell Father that the boots he wrote about would not be any good to me. I always wear high riding boots with high cowboy heels on them like a lady's shoe; they are very comfortable and the heels prevent one's foot from slipping through the stirrup. With regard to six shooter, a Colt's Frontier to take an American .44 cartridge is the best thing; I can get cartridges for either .44 or .45 American. I don't know which is the best size, some use one and some the other. Plated is better than blue as it does not rust so easily.

I have heard talk about Canon Hollard's son[19] being out here. He is close to this place but the account one hears of him here is very different to what you hear of him. He is one of the usual English sort who does nothing but play polo and drinks and plays the fool generally. His horse ranch is a myth. I believe he has some polo ponies and that is about all. The old canon came out here to pay his debts and his son fed him about as roughly as he could, so the old man did not stop long. I think young Hollard is going back to England soon.

Nearly all the Englishmen out here go on in the same way, pony racing, etc., and are the laughing stock of all the Americans. The article in Longmans on why the Englishman is a failure is quite true. The man knows what he is writing about but most of it applies more to the states and farming than it does to the cattle business. There is a lot of dancing here. They have a dance every week, also there is tennis playing, etc., but an Englishman that goes in for that sort of thing is considered no good. I must finish this letter I am writing it in the office at the Hudson's Bay. Hope Grandpa is better now.

The roundup is on now and it is raining like anything today. I am glad I am not out.

Hudson's Bay Company,
Macleod,
June 19, 1895,

My dear Mother,

I have bought a ranch. I bought it yesterday. It is the one I told you about that the H.B. Co. had a mortage on. I am now the owner of 160 acres of land, 80 acres of which is under crop. The rest is good grass ground. There is a good spring on it and one that is not so good. I have a house with 4 rooms and a kitchen in it, a small one-roomed house, 3 cellars and 1 big root cellar, 8 horse stable, granary, calf house, cow barn, yard, etc. The whole place is fenced. My crop consists of about 60 acres of oats, 5 potatoes, 2 rye, 6 wheat, and 5 barley. I am not quite certain of the exact acreage.

The H.B. Co. had a mortage on the place for $1,400 and they have had to pay Dunbar,[20] the occupant $350 for the crop as I would not buy the place unless I had the crop on it. I have paid $1,500 for the whole business, crop and all, so I think I have not done so badly. The ranch is always spoken of as one of the best in the country. It was one of the first taken up so the man had the whole country to choose from when he took his location. I have plenty of room to put you up next year. I am going to live in the small house for a little bit till the Dunbars are able to move out of the other house. Dunbar, the late owner of the place, is an old man and is very ill so I cannot fire him out neck and crop and I do not want to as they have been very decent about giving up the ranch and have made no bother. It seems hard on the old man as his sons got him into debt. I shall be busy now buying horses, cattle, machinery, etc.

I must hurry up and finish this as it is post time. I am now a landed proprietor and have quite an estate. What I want now is plenty of rain to make my stuff grow; we suffer from drought in this country.

P.S. You see the H.B. Co. are out of pocket by the sale as they are out three years' interest as well as the $250. My address is still Macleod. The ranch is 17 miles from town.

Springfield Ranch,
July 7, 1895,

My dear Mother,

This is the first letter from my new home. I should have written before but I have been so busy riding about the country buying horses and fixing things that I have had no time.

I have bought a team of horses from Jim Bell that are fairly light. I want them to do all the light work about the place, drive to town, run in the mower, etc. They cost me $125. One is a chestnut 4-year-old called "Captain" and the other a light bay 3-year-old called "Major." They are half-bred Clyde horses, both broken to saddle, and Bell broken them to harness for me. Then I bought a team from the Waldron Ranch.[21] They are purebred Clydes, dark brown, stand about 15 hands and weigh about 1,300 lbs. each. They are nice, low set, heavy mares. I intend breeding from them. They are as alike as two peas, only one has a white hind foot on the right side and the other on the left. They are 4 years old and are being broken to harness. They cost me $160 which is not dear taking all things into consideration. I think they will make a splendid team. I have not got them home yet. Then I bought a saddle horse from Franklin. It is a chestnut, 4 years old, broken to picket and hobbles, and is good to ride—at least it does not buck. I don't care what else it does. I saw Franklin break it while I was with Bell. It has only been ridden a few times and is, of course, raw yet but I think it will make a good horse. It cost me $50. My horses ought to be growing into money for the next year or two as they are all broncos only broke this spring. I have bought a wagon and harness. The wagon cost $125 and the harness $78, the four horse set.

I brought the things out on Thursday. I had a fine show starting—new wagon and harness, and a pair of horses. Mr. Gigot was rather scared as my horses have only been driven for the first time on Sunday and he thought I was going to break my neck. I told him that they went perfectly quiet but, of course, they were rather scared being in town for the first time. They went off very quietly indeed like a pair of old horses, which was rather disappointing after the fuss that was made when I started. They have continued going quietly like a pair of old horses.

I have a man working for me now during haymaking and harvest. I want someone as there is a lot of work to do. I am fencing a pasture field for my horses and I have 6 acres of potatoes to ridge up and a lot to do in the garden. We start haymaking on the 20th of this month. The man's name is Bill McClintock. He is a pretty good all round man.

My crop is looking very well. I have some rye out in ear; it stands nearly 3 foot 6 inches high. I have some barley in ear also. We have had a lot of rain in the last 2 or 3 days. It has done a lot of good and there is a very good prospect of them being a good crop. I hope there will be and that it will fetch a good price. I have not bought my cattle yet as I have not heard of any to quite suit me. Most of the bunches cost rather more money than I can lay out. I think there is money for me to buy weaner steers every year. I can buy them for from $10 to $12 and sell them when they are 4 years old at $40. Of course, one has to wait 4 years when there is nothing coming in, but when it does come, it comes in a lump. But the 4 years of waiting is very hard as one's expenses are going on all the time. Of course, if I got a mixed bunch I would get a return from them every year which is encouraging but I would have to pay a proportionate price for them, which is as broad as it is long in the end. I think I have got a very fair bargain in this ranch as everyone speaks very well of it.

If the weather is fine I am going up after a load of poles tomorrow for my fence.

———————————

Porcupine Hills,
July 22, 1895,

My dear Mother,

I have had a busy time lately and shall now have the next two months for haymaking and harvesting. I think I shall have a good crop as it is looking very well and the weather has been very favourable for growing. There has been a lot of rain. I have had my two mares brought down from the Waldron. They look very nice. Everyone who sees them admires them very much. One is called "Midget" and the other "Birdie." I have not been able to drive them yet as I have not had time but I hope to do so this afternoon.

I went into town on Friday and bought a mowing machine and horse rake. I hope to start cutting tomorrow. I also took out a cattle and horse brand. My brand is G "G 7 Combined" (my number at school used to be 7, that was one reason for choosing it). I brand on the left ribs for cattle and the right jaw for horses. I like a jaw brand for horses as it does not spoil their appearance like those brands on the shoulder or hip. I have bought 5 head of cattle from Sam Dunbar. One is a red mottled cow, gentle to milk, a steer calf, and 3 yearling steers.

July 28th. I got this far when I had to quit and I have not had time to write any more until today, neither have I had an opportunity to post it. I am expecting Hunter out from town today and he will post it for me tomorrow. I am very busy putting up hay. I do the cutting and I have two men raking and hauling it in with a 4 horse team. Out in the field one man takes the 2 leaders and rakes while the other takes the wheelers and loads. I had to get his 2nd man (his name is McAllister) with his horses as when I started to drive my mares I found that they were too coltish to drive together in a mowing machine so I drive them one at a time with a gentle horse. It is no joke being run away with a mowing machine. My mares have only been driven a few times and they acted very lively with me the time I drove them together in the wagon. Everyone tells me that I have the best team anywhere round here. I think I shall show them in Macleod the fall at the show.

I have insured myself against accidents to the extent of $5 a week in the event of being killed, $1,000 in Bab's favour. So she has an interest in that amount in how the colts behave and as all my horses are colts she has a good chance for her money. I have done well with that money in the Funds; it has paid good interest. You know the things I want sent out—flannel shirts with collar, pants, blankets (coloured ones), and socks, only get them warm enough. I have those scarves you sent last year. I must try and get a fur overcoat if my crop turns out well. They cost $49 but one has to have one.

Macleod,
August 11, 1895,

My dear Mother and Aunt,

I have received indignant letters from both of you telling me that you have been 3 weeks without a letter. I cannot help that; you must blame the post office. I write once a fortnight which I think is pretty fair. I wanted to write to Aunt Nellie today but as I am so busy this letter will have to do you both. I am busy all the week cutting hay. I drive the mowing machine. I get up early, round the horses in, have breakfast, then Bill and I grind the machine knives. Then I go out, taking my lunch with me, and I do not get back till after 8 at night. Then as soon as I have eaten I go to bed. Today (Sunday), part of this morning I have been shelling peas for our dinner and after dinner I have to go over to Sam Dunbar's on business.

We had 2 days rain this week and I went to town on the second day (Friday). I had heard that there were some cattle for sale at Lethbridge and I went to see about his cattle he told me he wanted to sell. He had borrowed money on his cattle and wanted to get out of debt (he was paying 24% on it I expect as that is the interest they charge here on borrowed money). In the end, after seeing Mr. Gigot (Black works for the H.B. Co. in Macleod), I bought all the cattle that he and his brother can round up in the fall at $20 a head, this year's calves to be thrown in. He expects there will be about 125 head. They are a mixed bunch so I shall have some beef to sell from them next year. They are nearly all young cattle 2, 3, & 4, but very few 1-year-olds. The 2's are worth $20, 3's and 4's more in proportion, and the 1's are worth $15. As there are considerably more 3 & 4 than 1 they will be all right for the price. This year's calves are worth $10; there will be about 30 of them that he will give me. The cattle are well bred and as good as any on the range.

I have bought about all the things I want to now. I intend to put up about 50 ton of hay if I get time; I have to go about 7 miles for it. The crop is looking well. We have had one of the wettest and most growing seasons that they have had for years. I am using the potatoes grown in my garden.

Please tell Aunt Nellie that Macleod is full of stores that sell everything. There is the H.B. Co., Barker, Miller & Gardiner (no relation of ours but the junction of names is funny), Reach & Co., Ryan & Co., and several others. With regards to my house which seems to be worrying you, I expect you would be disappointed if you saw it. It is built of logs but they are warm and we don't trouble much about houses in the Wild West. The colts are working well, no accidents owing to my being insured.

Macleod,
September 2, 1895,

My dear Mother,
Just a few lines to let you know I am all right and everything is lovely. I will have a chance to send this is on Wednesday. I had no chance till now and you could hardly expect me to ride 40 miles and lose a day in order to post a letter. I have finished haymaking and have put up about 40 tons, I think. I am now busy harvesting. I should have been carrying some oats that I cut green for feed today, only the wind is so bad that we could not pitch grain in it so I have been making a corral for my calves. I have quite a bit of corral building to do. I am building these of unedged boards and battening the cracks with slabs. It will make a good strong shed.

Yesterday was the first day of prairie chicken shooting and being Sunday we took a day and went shooting. We ran across 2 coveys and we killed 5 birds. McClintock has got his wife and family out here now. I have put them to live in the kitchen of the house. I am still living in the shack and shall be till old Mr. and Mrs. Dunbar move out. Their new house over at Sam Dunbar's ranch is not finished yet. Mrs. McClintock does the cooking for me, that is why I let McClintock bring her out. She is a very good cook and used to cook in a hotel in Winnipeg. It saves a lot of time having her to do the cooking as, of course, while a man is messing around the house he cannot be doing any work.

If you are going to send me out any blankets you had better hurry up and send them as I am wanting some now as the weather is pretty cold. I shall be glad when I get the harvest in as we shall soon have the snow about. I do not know anyone who wants a pupil or who would take young Arnett. If he is earning enough to keep him at home he will do much better there than out here and have a much nicer life.

We have a stray dog round here who is a kind of retriever but a more useless brute never lived. I tried him at the chickens yesterday but he would not hunt and if we try to drive stock he generally runs the wrong ones. I shall draw my six shooter and kill him one of these days if he does not look out. No more time.

Macleod,
September 19, 1895,

My dear Mother,

I am going on the roundup the day after tomorrow most likely. I do not know how long I shall be away as I am going to get my cattle. I am going into town tomorrow to make arrangements. I have bought a saddle horse. I have 2 now. I am going to try and get along with only them but I may have to get another 1 or 2 if I find that the work is too much for them. I gave $50 or £10 for this one. He is a bigger horse than the one I got before. I bought a fur coat the other day the H.B. Co. store. It is a very good coon skin coat. Gigot said it was from selected skins made to order for someone. The price of it was $60 only Gigot sold it to me for $50. I was much amused at Aunt Nellie talking about a *fur-lined coat*. Our coats here are made of fur and lined with quilting. You have the fur outside, you know.

Since I wrote last we have had a fall of snow which lasted on the ground for about a day and knocked my grain down as if it had been rolled. It made me feel very blue but most of it has got up again so I hope it has not been damaged very much. I hope to have it cut in a day or two. I have some of it cut and carried. I wish it all was. We have been having a lot of wind lately which is almost as bad as snow or rain as one cannot work with the grain or hay in the wind. You do not know what wind is in England.

I hope you have sent off my things. I am wanting them and have put off buying warm things till I get them and see what you have sent. I am scribbling this off in a hurry as I am very busy. I will write you again as soon as I get off the roundup and tell you how many cattle I got. Tell Father not to bring his bike when he comes to see me. I prefer a horse. I cannot understand anyone who has ridden a horse riding one of those things.

I am getting on with my corral building when I cannot work at the grain. There is now a regular blizzard and snowstorm on and has been for the last 36 hours. The thermometer must be down to nearly zero and the wind cuts my face like a knife, even with a cap over my ears.

Porcupine Hills,
October 13, 1895,

My dear Mother,

I have just come off the roundup. I have been away much longer than I expected. I have had turned over to me 66 head of big stock, which I have to pay for, and 25 calves which are thrown in. This makes 91 head and, with the 5 head I had before, makes me the owner of 96 head of cattle which is very near 100. The cattle I got from Black were very cheap. I was offered $5 a head on my bargain. Reed offered me $12 each for my steer calves which would have made the cows cost me only $8 but I want the steers as bad as he does. I had 40 cows turned over, all nice young ones, and 4 bulls. I had 13 two-years and 3 one-year steers turned over. I can sell the 5 three-years next year for $40 each and so double my money on them in one year and I may be able to sell quite a few of the 2-year-olds then too. We had good weather on the roundup but it was very cold, especially at night. We were called at ½ past 4 and would be out and had breakfast, caught the horses, and ridden some miles before ever it was daylight. We came back in at the middle of the day to change horses and eat, then ride again till dark. If there was not a corral handy, or the herd was too big for it, we had to take reliefs at night herding them. It depends on the size of the herd as to how many men are on at a time but as a general rule it is from 2 to 4. The first relief is from about 8 to 10, the next from 10 to 1, then 1 to 3, and 3 to 5 or 6. I was only on one night from 10 to 1; that is the worst shift as you get your night's rest in 2 pieces. You get nicely to sleep and then you have to go out and ride, and when you get to sleep again it is time to get up. People write all sorts of rot about it but I fail to see the beauty of riding round and round a herd of cattle in the moonlight with the thermometer nearly at zero singing the beggars to sleep, especially if they don't want to sleep and want to eat or stampede. We had beef and cows and calves in the herd. The cows and calves are all right but the beef is hard to herd.

On a roundup one man is chosen captain and all the rest are under his orders. Cowboys, or punchers as we are called, would make a good irregular cavalry as there is as much discipline as in an army. We had a few bucking horses along but did not have any good shows. There was a young Irishman with us just out from the Old Country and his bronco piled him one day in fine style. It fired him right over its head and he lit on his back on the ground. It is the only time I have seen a man genuinely fired like that.

I did not have half enough saddle horses but I managed to make out but I brought my horses back like bags of bones. One ought never to have less than 8 out with him as the work is very hard on horses.

I brought the parcel out from town with me as I came through. I had to pay £2 duty on the things but they had never been opened. I had to swear all sorts of things and kiss the book at the customs house in Macleod. The drawers are good and warm but they seem very dear. The shirts seem to have cost a lot of money; those that I brought out with me cost $6 each at the A & N and seem to be as thick as wool or thicker. The next lot you bring I want all grey ones; they look much nicer and last clean longer. It does not matter how coarse they are as they wear longer than fine ones. I am amused at the ties. I have not worn a tie since I have been out here. We always wear a handkerchief tied round our necks, silk if one can afford it, but I always wear a coloured cotton one, an imitation bandana. I should look a dude in those shirts and ties. The blankets are much cheaper than we get here. I had to get another pair before the roundup. I got the cheapest I could as I was expecting these. It cost me $5 a pair. All blankets here are made in pairs, not divided into single ones. The pair I got are much heavier than those you sent. You better get some to bring with you; get some that go about 8 lbs. to the pair. Don't get red ones as only Indians use red ones. You had better bring several pairs.

On the roundup I used 3 pair, a railway macintosh, old Volunteer overcoat, a fur coat, and a tarpaulin sheet for a bed. I slept in nearly all my clothes as we always do when it is cold. You had better bring clothes for all kinds of weather. It may be hot or it may be cold when you are here. One cannot tell for 2 hours what the weather will be like. It has not been hot this year at all. Nearly all my grain has been frozen and I shall not have much to sell. But it will do to feed in the straw unthrashed. I have a lot of barley but cannot get the weather to get in in. It either snows or the wind blows so hard that we cannot work straw in it.

I am getting my potatoes in now. I have a lot of Indians working on the job. They take their wages out in potatoes. I had one lot come and after a day's work they wanted cash but did not get it. I paid them in potatoes for what they did and they left. Then this lot came on and have agreed to dig them out for potatoes. I cannot afford to pay cash as one gets so little for the potatoes.

I expected to find a six shooter in the parcel that Father talked about but there is plenty of time yet for it to arrive. I must finish this long letter now and hope for better weather before I write again.

Porcupine Hills,
October 27, 1895,

My dear Mother,

Since writing my last letter to you I have done the harvest. It did not take very long to get the grain in. I got hold of plenty of help and made the most of the fine weather that we had. I got Sam Dunbar to lend me a man and wagon and Jim Dunbar came on with a wagon so we had 3 wagons going in the field and pulled in about 24 loads a day.

I had got this far with the letter when Hunter came out and I have not had time to touch it for a week. Last week I branded all the calves that were not branded and a few cattle that I had bought before. We had quite a little roundup on our own account. I got a young fellow called Jim Ferguson to come and rope for me and Jim Dunbar lent me a hand. Young MacAllister had 4 to brand so he came and helped McClintock, the man who is working for me, so we had quite a party. But we needed them all as some of the cattle were pretty strong. I had one big cow to brand; we threw her down and laid her there with our ropes and I put my iron on her all right. I have now 94 head of cattle with my brand on.

We had a beast of a snow storm last night and the cattle all look pretty cold today, ditto myself. I have an Indian herding my cattle for me for a bit till I get my work done, which I hope will be soon. He is a good man. I had him digging post holes one time. He takes a lot of trouble over the cattle which most of the beggars will not do when the weather is bad. It is amusing to talk to him as I know only a few words of Indian and have to make signs to him and shout at him. He was away for a week the other day. It was treaty time with the Indians when they get paid their treaty money. They have great times then and have a lot of horse racing, betting and gambling till it is all spent. It seems a great farce that the country should pay these men a lot of money every year that they may have a good time. They cannot get any drink as there is a big fine and imprisonment to anyone selling or giving whiskey to Indians.

I shall be glad when the threshing machine comes and threshes out the little grain that I have that is fit to thresh. I will take this letter out with me when I go riding this afternoon and see if I can find anyone going to town that I may get it posted. I have only been there once since I came off the roundup. I don't go to town oftener than I can help as I cannot afford the expense. My potatoes are all up and in the cellar.

Porcupine Hills,
November 25, 1895,

My dear Mother,

Since writing my last letter I have threshed the little grain I have worth threshing. I got 22½ bushels of rye, 110 of barley, 27 oats and 145 wheat. The rye was grown from one bushel of seed and I keep it all for next year as it makes very good feed. The barley was grown on 3 acres and the wheat on 5 acres so it did not yield so bad, considering the oats was a load that had been put at the bottom of one of the stacks. It took a day and a half to thresh but that was owing to there being a very heavy crop of straw which took a long time to go through the machine. The rest of my grain I am going to feed to the cattle just as it is in the straw. It is so pinched with the frost that it will not be worth threshing; anyway, the price of grain is so bad that it is hardly worth the expense of threshing which is very heavy. In addition to paying the men you have to feed them and 14 men eat quite a bit of grub.

I have bought 36 head of young steers (23 calves and 13 yearlings and 2-year-olds. They will I hope grow into beef in time and will be worth some money, $40 a head. They cost me $12 a head for the calves and $17 for the yearlings and 2-year-olds, and they will be beef at 4-year-olds I hope. I have a great deal of feed so I want plenty of stock to eat it. I have weaned my calves and the cows are at present bawling round the corral, trying to get at them. I have 53 calves in the corral that I am feeding; most of them are steers, some I got from Black and the last lot I bought. I have now all the cattle I can afford to buy—130 head in all, or rather, 132 with 2 I have not branded yet. They are all doing well and I hope they will continue to do so.

At present we are having bad weather. The thermometer has been below zero and the ground is covered with snow. We are hard at work building a ditch to run the water from the spring through the corrals. I am going to run the water inside logs, I have the logs all ready for the man to bore and we are digging the ditch to put them in. Then I have a shed to build and most of my work will be done. I shall not have to pay anyone then for I will do the rest of my work myself.

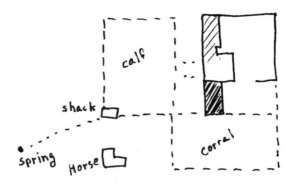

I enclose a plan of my ranch. The dotted lines are what I have built this fall. As you will see, the small corral was already built. The ink spot is the shed I have to build. The line of the water from the spring is shown. The shaded portion is my building, stable, etc. In the left is the house and the shack I have been living in. The big main corral is where I keep the big stock. The calf corral is where the calves run in the day and they sleep in the old corral. The stacks are all in the middle corral so are handy to feed. I am in the house now. We moved in yesterday. I will give you a plan of the house.

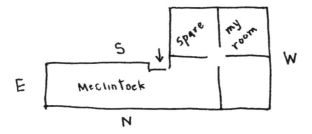

Where McClintock lives is by rights the kitchen. The two rooms which serve as kitchen and spare room are really one and I shall knock out the partition next spring before you come. Also I will make the dining room with the bedrooms opening off it. By the by, bring some insect poison as you may need it. These log buildings are great for visitors. I am going to tear all the canvas and paper off the walls and ceiling before you come and will whitewash and put up new for you. I cannot do it now as the weather is cold.

I must get you to raise a subscription to buy a democrat buggy to drive you in when you come out; it will cost about $150. I will pay some if I can get you to put in some of it. I could not very well drive you about in a heavy wagon without springs. It would look very bad, besides being uncomfortable for you. A democrat is a useful trap; it is a 4-wheeled rig and one can carry quite a lot of things on it. Most people use them as you can bring out grub from town which one cannot do in a fancy rig. I hope we shall be able to manage it.

Can Bab ride yet? I shall get her a nice pony. I shall have no difficulty about that as I know some people called Arnold who raise horses. They have several girls who ride and break horses and they can be trusted to have a good quiet one or two. I asked one of the boys the other day if they had any and showed me on that was as quiet as could possibly be imagined, nothing would frightened it. Bab must ride if she ever wants to leave the house as one cannot walk any distance, especially a woman, on account of the wild cattle. They do not understand anyone on foot and are apt to be inquisitive, which is not pleasant.

I hear the wind getting up a little. I hope we are going to have a chinook.

Dec. 1—I have a chance to post this letter at last. We are having a cold storm. All my big cattle drifted off yesterday and I am going out now to hunt them up. I hope I shall get them.

Porcupine Hills
December 12, 1895,

My dear Father,

I have received the gun all right and like it very much. I have not fired it yet, not having been to town to get cartridges. I have got nearly all my cattle back again now except 1 cow and a calf and 2 steers. I shall run across them somewhere and they won't hurt anyway as they don't want feeding. We have had a cold spell of weather but it is better now. We had the thermometer down to 20 below zero, 28 below in Macleod, which is pretty cold I tell you. One hates to leave the fire when it is like that.

We had a shooting scrape close to here the other day. A man called Lemar, the foreman of the Waldron Ranch Co., shot a man called Mackoy twice, once in the leg and the next shot in the shoulder. Mackoy's gun misfired both times, bad for Mackoy. Mackoy went down there on purpose to shoot Lemar, so it appears. He called in here on his way down but did not say anythng about his intentions.[23] My ranch is right in the middle of the Waldron lease; they are a big company and own about 10,000 head of cattle. Their lease is up next year, I am glad to say, not that they trouble me much but they certainly make themselves unpleasant to some of the neighbours.

Last Sunday my next neighbour was run in by the Police on the suspicion of having taken some wood from an old hut belonging to the Waldron between his place and mine. But they let him out again as they could not find any evidence against him. He is now vowing that he is going to go after the Waldron for malicious arrest.

Did I tell you that we nearly had a prairie fire here when I was on the roundup? It was let out by a party of men putting up hay for the Waldron and burnt quite a bit of ground but they managed to get it out. If there had been a wind blowing they could not have done so; it would have come this way and most likely burnt me out. I am glad they stopped it. I am insured.

We are· having a son-of-a-gun of a wind now; it blows enough to knock one off a horse. It is always doing something out here.

Porcupine Hills
December 18, 1895,

My dear Father,

The man who sold you that gun does not know his business. it has been made for the English market and will only take a .455 cartridge, which is an English one. There may be a .45 cartridge made that is as short as the .455 but the ordinary .45 is much longer. The tracing that I have enclosed is from the picture that was on the box the gun came in and is the exact size of a .45 cartridge. The arrow shows how far it will go into the cylinder. The inside of the cylinder is only bored as far as a .455 cartridge goes in, but not as far as the .45 goes. The consequence is that a .45 will go in so far and then it sticks. It seems a peculiar thing that they should put a picture of a .45 cartridge on the lid of the box and the gun inside will not take that cartridge, but this is the case. On the end of the box where the bore of the gun is marked, they have pasted a piece of paer over the .45 and have written on it .455. The gun also is marked .455. I may be able to get the chambers in the cylinder bored down further so that it will take a .45 or I can return the cylinder or the whole gun.

I would ask you to see the A & N people and hear what they have to say on the matter. It is entirely their fault that this mistake has been made and they certainly ought to pay for their mistakes. I hope I have explained the matter plainly. You can understand that in shooting coyotes and wolves one wants to use the long cartridge as it will carry further. Besides, they only keep the ordinary .44 & .45 cartridges out here. I will not do anything in the matter till I hear from you. Please excuse my writing as I am writing on a chair and I cannot get it steady.

[No date]

My dear Mother,

It is a long time I am afraid since my last letter so I must hurry up and get this one off. I did not go anywhere at Christmas but kept at home, saw nobody, and the day was almost the same as any other. I have been very busy lately. I have my spring fixed now the water is running all right. I fired McClintock as soon as I got it done. I wish I could have done it sooner but the man who did the pipes (MacFarquer) smashed his auger that he was going to use to bore the logs with and had to send east for a new one. Besides, the weather was very bad which hindered him. McClintock is living in part of my house and will be there all the winter; his wife cooks for me. Billy Smith is still with me but I don't pay him anything. He gets his grub. He helps me feed my cattle and makes it not so lonely as if I was by myself. Besides, I could not leave the ranch if I had no one there to feed things when I was away.

I have to go over to the Kootenay River soon, I think this week if the weather is fine. I have several head of cattle over at Black's place and I want to see them and get Stevens to look after them for me this winter. He sent me word that he had them. I cannot bring them over till the spring as the days are too short now to drive cattle such a long journey.

We have had all sorts of weather. We had it down to 36° below zero in Macleod, in some places below 40, and within 24 hours the wind changed to the west and we had a Chinook and water running. That is an awful change in temperature in 24 hours because it has to be quite a bit above freezing point, as you know, to melt snow and ice in a hurry. I think it is rather hard on one such sudden changes in the temperature. It gave me a beast of a cold but I am getting better. It has got cold again, now nearly to zero I should think, but that is not bad if it does not go much below and the wind does not blow. The wind makes all the difference. When it is from the north it is cold as blazes and from the west it is as a rule warm. When it is cold, like it was the other day, one hates to leave the stove but one has to feed the cattle. You have to look out not to get frostbitten. I froze the top of my nose just going from the stable to the house. It is a funny sensation. You feel it sting for a minute and then it is all over. It goes white and you feel nothing at all till you thaw out. That is the worst of it; if you don't notice the sting you get frozen without knowing it.

You ask what to bring with you. Well you had better bring your bedding, blankets and sheets, etc. Sheets are unknown in the Wild West. I expect you had better bring a few cups and saucers and plates; mine are all enameled iron. You can get those things in Montreal or Toronto or somewhere. There is a good shop in Toronto called Eatons; it is a kind of Shroolbreds. Let me know if you are going there and I will have you get me an outfit of grub. It is much cheaper at Eatons than it is up here.

If ever you go by Potters would you get his price for riding boots and whether he can make me a pair with the measures he has or whether he would want any more. If he makes them cheaper than I get them made out here I will get you to bring me a pair.

My cattle are doing well so far. Did I ever tell you how I was going to fix my spring? I have had a 1¾-inch hole bored through the centre of pine logs and they make the pipes. The logs are 11 feet long; it comes cheaper than iron pipes. My spring just keeps that hole full all the time. I will run a pipe into the house when you are here, I think, but I will talk over it with you and get your advice.

———————

Porcupine Hills
February 10, 1896,

My dear Mother,

I am living all alone now and am in consequence up to my eyes in work. I am cooking at the present time, engaged in baking bread, but I am afraid I have not got a very good scale on it as the dough will not rise well. Smith has gone to the Indian Agency to cook for Nash, the agent. Nash's girl had left him and his wife does not cook. He could not hear of another girl so they thought they would try a man cook. Smith is a good cook so they sent for him and he was glad to get a job. You know he was only staying with me not getting any pay.

I went into town last Monday week. There was a theatrical company in town so I went to the theatre. I had not been anywherer for a long time so I think the extravagance was justified, especially as I was away only one night. I left McClintock to look after the cattle; you know he was living in part of my house and his wife was cooking for me. When I came out I found he had not fed the big stock that night (he said he did not think they wanted feeding) so I had a row with him and told him he had better clear out, which he did with his outfit. My real reason for getting rid of him was that it was too expensive having them round. I was keeping them in coal and oil and I used to think that his wife used some of my grub, at least all the bread seemed to be made from my flour sack. It was the same with other things so I thought I had better take the first opportunity of making a change. One can pay too much for having one's food cooked I thought.

I hope I shall get someone to come and stay with me for the rest of the winter. There are always a lot of men glad to get somewhere to stop for their grub in the winter. It is pretty lonely by one's self and not over safe as one might get hurt and no one would know about it for a long time. It is more lonely here than where I was last winter. Reed and Patterson lived closer than any of my neighbours do now and the men over there were all cowboys and we used to ride a good bit together, but here there is no one who rides the range at all. My neighbours are all small men with but a few cattle which stop right round them so they do not have to ride after them. I had a calf born a day or two ago. It is the first calf I have had since I started. It is nice and healthy but it is very early to have any yet as the weather is so cold for them. The beginning of April is quite soon enough.

There was a dance down the creek the other day; the woman who does my washing, or rather her daughter, gave it. I went to it. It sounds rather funny going to a dance at your wash woman's but that cuts no figure out here.

When you come out could you bring me a cartridge loading outfit? It is only a small machine; you can see one at the stores. I want it to load 12-bore cartridges; it ought to cost about $10 or perhaps not as much. There is a powder measure, a rammer, and a turnover machine in the outfit. Of course, when you go through the customs you should say the things you have are *settlers effects*. If you have any overweight, it can come cheaper by rail if you say it is *settlers effects*. Could you bring me over a box of Egyptian cigarettes; they are unobtainable out here except at a prohibitive price. You could open the box and take a few out and say you smoked them yourself if the Customs people see them, but the chances are if you tell them you are coming out to settle they won't look at your luggage. They never opened mine.

I hope it will not be cold tomorrow as I want to take some potatoes down to Hollies that I have sold him. I will take this letter down at the same time as he often goes into town to get things for his store. He keeps a small trading store about three miles below here and married a Miss Dunbar. You cannot take potatoes out in the cold, you know, or they will freeze.

Hudson's Bay Company,
Macleod,
March 1, 1896,

My dear Father,

I got your letter about the 6 shooter all right. I think I can fix it all right here. The Police use an English gun (the Enfield revolver) which takes an English .45 cartridge and I can get some cartridges out of them. They fit my gun as I tried some in it the other day.

I had a touch of the D----- influenza again and have been seedy for the last 3 weeks. I had to come into town last Wednesday and when I saw the doctor he took my temperature and felt my pulse and told me I ought not to be out of doors. My temperature was 104° and pulse was 122 so he gave me an order for a physic and I have to stop in town till Sunday. I am much better now; my temperature yesterday had fallen to 101° and is steadily going down but the doctor says I must not try to work for another week or 10 days, not till I am thoroughly well, or I shall be as bad again. I am staying in the H.B. Co.'s place with Hunter, the bookkeeper, and get my meals at the hotel. I want to leave town as soon as I can so I will try it tomorrow if the cold moderates. It is too expensive in here—50 cents a meal, livery stable bill for my horse, doctor's bill, and chemist's bill. I don't know how much this little amusement has let me in for, confound it. It has turned pretty cold since I have been in town and is 5 below zero now at ½ past ten in the morning. It went down to 15 below last night.

There is a young fellow called Murray staying on the ranch with me now till he hears of a job. I was quite alone for a bit until he came along and agreed to stay with me and help me for his grub till he heard of a job. He lived close to me last winter on the Kootenay. I guess he wonders what has become of me if Hollies has not driven up and told him.

Tell Bab if she does not know how to ride before she comes out, it does not matter. The girls out here will teach her and she can get her riding habit much cheaper here as they don't go in for expensive rigs in the Colonies. We'll borrow a saddle out here. But tell them to dismiss from their minds that they will be able to drive themselves about. Neither of them could handle a pair of young horses up and down the steep hills and neither of them could even work the brake.

Tell Mother she can get all the groceries she wants here in the H.B. Co. store. They are as fresh as any she gets in London and mostly the same brands. Cross and Blackwell, Coleman mustard, and all the rest of it, *only the prices are higher.* But I have come to the conclusion that she had better buy here than down East, owing to the high freight charges. Ask her if she means to insult me by saying she wants a *clean* saucepan; does she think mine are dirty? We are always very particular to have a wash up of all plates, dishes, and cooking utensils after evrey meal. Tell her also if she wants to go across the Rocky Mountains she had better buy her ticket in London. If she bought it here she would find it would cost her more than she paid for the whole of her journey. That is one of the little jokes of the CPR; you can buy a ticket in London to come out here for about half the price they charge you here for one to London. I believe that the pass through the Rockies is very fine but you have to take a 90% discount off the descriptions in a CPR pamphlet. Of course, I lived about 5 miles from the foot of them and one sees them every day so one gets rather tired of them as samples of scenery. They are as barren and desolate as a pile of rocks can be.

I have to put a new floor into my house before Mother comes as the old one is rotten and full of holes. I am thinking of putting down cedar flooring grooved and tongued and nailing it over the old floor to save buying joists. I think it will be warmer too. Then I have to fill the spaces between the logs afresh as the mud is falling out. I shall use lime and sand as it lasts longer than mud, though of course it costs more. I will try and pull out to the ranch tomorrow as I am nearly all right now and feel pretty fit.

Macleod,
March 16, 1896

My dear Mother,

In my last letter home which was written to Father I told you I was in town and the doctor would not let me come out. I stayed in town for a week when I felt all right and came out here again. I am all right now. I am still taking a tonic that the doctor gave me but there is nothing wrong now. I am going into town tomorrow with a wagon to get the lime to plaster the chinks in the house. I shall go in again next day and get the lumber for the floor, then we shall set to work and do the house up. Don't be afraid; you will not be obliged to sleep on a heap of sacking or hay as you seem to expect. I am going to buy an iron bedstead for you (it is better than a wood one in the country) with a spring mattress and if you don't like springs I will let you have my wood one and use the springs myself.

In my last letter I said I thought we had better get what we want at the H.B. Co. in Macleod. Their things are as good as you can get anywhere and when you take the freight into consideration about as cheap. Besides it will not do for me to offend the H.B. as they are my bankers as well and I cannot be independent for a couple of years.

We had a beast of a storm while I was in town. It went down to 32° below zero and it snowed quite a lot. I had 3 cows die during the storm. One was an old cow, the oldest I had. I had been feeding her all the winter and she seemed as well as possible when I went into town but she was dead when I got home. Murray said he never noticed anything the matter with her at all at night and he found her dead in the morning. The other two died from weakness. We had about 3 weeks of warm weather before and the cattle had begun to shed their winter coats and the consequence was the sudden cold knocked them out. Everybody lost a few during that storm but that is not much consolation to me.

You can buy butter here. I use it right along, good creamery butter too. I will try and rustle a milk cow. I had intended milking the old one that died as she was broken to milk but I shall have to break one of my wild ones or buy or borrow a gentle one. Potter's price for boots is much too high. I can get them made to order here for $8 or ready made for $5. I shall plant every kind of vegetable I can think of in the garden but it will most likely be a little after you get here before they will be fit to use. Until they are, we must use potatoes and tinned vegetables which are very nice and fresh and good.

P.S. Have you learnt how to make plum cake? I am doing my own cooking now. Murray and I run the cook stove together but since I have not been well I have been doing all the cooking and he the work outside.

Macleod,
April 12, 1896

My dear Mother,

I hope that this letter will reach you before you leave. I am going near town tomorrow to hunt up my horses who have got away from me and will try and post this then. You ask me in one of your letters what things I have in the way of knives and forks so I will send you an inventory of what I have: 6 knives, 6 forks made of steel with white handles, 6 teaspoons, 3 table-spoons made of white metal, 4 tea cups and saucers made of enamel iron, and 6 enamel plates. My outfit though strong is not very swell.

I have been very busy with my house lately; Murray and I are nearly through. We have put new tar paper all over the roof, taken all the mud out of the cracks and filled them up again with mortar made of lime and sand whitewashed it outside and I am going to do the same inside. We have put down a new floor. It is the most expensive, B.C. cedar grooved and tongued flooring which makes a nice smooth floor. I will cotton your bedroom. The whole business will cost about $40. I don't know what I shall do for furniture; I have a bedroom set but my dining room outfit consists of 6 wood chairs and a *small* round table.

I think that I have told you before that you will have no trouble about butter as we use it all the time; it is plentiful and cheap. Vegetables will not be fit to use when you come but will be soon after. I have oceans of potatoes though, and with the tinned truck we get I think you will be able to manage all right. I have invested in 12 hens and they are doing well; they lay over 6 eggs a day. Yesterday I got 10. I don't feed them anything; they pick up the grain that is scattered about the yard. I hope to hatch out some chickens for Bab to look after so she had better come prepared. Also mind and bring some *new* music, latest songs and dances; one is very much behind the times in those things out here.

I hope to start ploughing in a few days, as soon as I get through with the house. I have 6 young calves now. I had to kill one the other day; it got its leg broke and it could not get up itself and suffered a lot of pain. I also had a cow die, which was a big loss. She was rather weak and, of course, had to go and mire herself down in the creek. I got her out and kept her alive for several days but she never got over it. The spring is very late in starting this year but it will most likely make up for it when it does begin. You will find it plenty warm enough when you get here.

Have you taken your ticket right through and return? Mind you do or you will regret it. They charge a lot more for the tickets out here than they do at home. Their object is to get people out here and when they get them they want to keep them.

[*Editor's note:* Claude Gardiner's mother and sister arrived in Fort Macleod about a month later. Not surprisingly, his long letters end at this point.].

Notes

1. Clarence C. Chipman (1856-1924) joined the civil service in 1867 and in 1882 he became private secretary to Sir Charles Tupper, later the prime minister of Canada. In 1884 he accompanied Tupper to London when the latter became High Commissioner for Canada in Great Britain. It was likely during this time that he came to know Gardiner's father and met young Claude. In 1891, Chipman joined the Hudson's Bay Co. as its chief commissioner, with headquarters in Winnipeg. He remained at that post until his retirement in 1911.
2. James W. Bell came west as a sub-constable in the North-West Mounted Police about 1874 and served most of his enlistment at Fort Macleod. Taking his discharge in 1879 he went into partnership with Robert Patterson, another ex-policeman, to establish one of Alberta's earliest ranches, located near Slideout, south-east of town. Bell married and had three children. At the time of his death in 1902, the *Macleod Gazette* commented that, "Mr. Bell has developed his cattle and horse business to very fair and comfortable dimensions, and was among the most prominent and prosperous individual owners in this part of the country. He was one of the solid men of the country, and a man who was thoroughly well liked and respected." (May 30, 1902).
3. The Cochrane Ranch was established by Senator M.H. Cochrane of Compton, Que., in 1881, and leased 109,000 acres of grazing land west of Calgary. However, a combination of bad weather and poor herding practises caused a major destruction of the first herds. Believing that the area was unsuited for cattle, the company moved in 1883 to a new site south-west of Fort Macleod. There it operated one of the biggest ranches in the West until until 1906, when it sold out to the Mormon Church. During much of its period in the Fort Macleod area, the senator's son, W.H. Cochrane, was the manager of the ranch.
4. Percy Kennard (1869-1946) was the son of an English physician. He came to western Canada alone as a teenager in 1886 and for the next eight years he worked on ranches near Fort Macleod. He then moved to the Cypress Hills in 1894 as a rider for the Cochrane Ranch. Three years later he started his own ranch near Elkwater Lake, remaining there until 1930, when he opened a general store and post office at Elkwater Lake.

5. This was the main ranch near Slideout. Bell's second ranch was located on the Waterton River, directly south of Pincher Creek. Likely it served only as a cow camp and grazing area to supplement the main ranching operations.

6. Claude's only sister, Barbara Gardiner, worked for many years for the St. John's Ambulance. As a young woman she had been engaged but her fiance was drowned and she never married. Instead, she remained a companion for her mother. During World War One she worked for St. John's Ambulance and settled in Bournemouth after the war. With her mother, she did an extensive amount of travelling during the interwar years, then rejoined the ambulance group at the outbreak of World War Two. During that conflict she suffered a minor shrapnel wound. She visited her relatives in western Canada twice after the war and died in the 1950s.

7. John Read (1861-1939) came west in 1883 and for the first six years he worked on I.G. Baker & Co.'s ranch in the Fort Macleod area. He was then employed on other ranches in southern Alberta and was with Bell at Slideout when Read married Eva Webb in 1893. Four years later, Read bought his own spread near Eagle Butte, near the Cypress Hills. In 1917 he left the cattle business and bought the Royal Hotel in Medicine Hat. In 1889, he participated in one of the first rodeos held in Alberta and won the steer roping event.

8. This may have been Dave Cochrane, a well known character who had a ranch near Standoff. He was an ex-policeman and was known for his unorthodox ways.

9. Robert Patterson (1855-1938) was born in Ireland and when he came to Canada in 1876 he immediately joined the North-West Mounted Police. He served most of his four years at Fort Macleod, and when he took his discharge he went into a ranching partnership with James Bell. He married Sarah Sayers in 1884, then dissolved his business partnership and went into ranching on his own. In 1886 he formed a new partnership with Richard Urch, operating ranches near Champion and Bassano. This partnership ended in 1906. In 1911, Patterson was elected a member of the Alberta legislature, representing the Macleod constituency as an Independent Conservative. He served a second term until 1917, when he returned to his original ranch at Slideout and remained there until his retirement.

10. Edwin Larkin (1852-1931) was born in Ireland and served in the North-West Mounted Police from 1874 to 1878. From the time of his discharge until the 1920s, he was reputed top be the finest roundup cook in southern Alberta. He cooked for many of the big ranches, included the Winder in 1878, the Walrond in 1879, and the Oxley for the next two years. In the 1880s and 1890s he was with the Cochrane, Circle, McFarlane, Bar U, and Mosquito Creek outfits. He also served in the Rocky Mountain Rangers during the Riel Rebellion of 1885. After the ranching era had passed, Larkin cooked for road crews, and hay camps.

11. Edward F. Gigot (1847-1928) was born in Mayence, Germany, and came to Canada at the age of seventeen. After being engaged in railway construction work, he joined the Hudson's Bay Co. in 1873, serving as branch manager at Portage La Prairie, Manitoba. In 1876, he married Rosa Ness and they had seven children. While in Manitoba in 1883, he was elected to the provincial legislature, representing St. Francois Xavier constituency. After a time in Manitoba, Gigot was transferred to Fort

Macleod where he was in charge of the H.B. Co. store and their other interests. In 1900 he moved to Nelson, B.C. where he remained until his retirement.

12. This may have been Louis Watson (1847-1933), who claimed to have been part of a caravan en route to the Tobacco Plains when he was born at the later site of Fort Macleod. He said his parents were killed in a raid and he was raised by Indians. He later married a Cree half-breed. He claimed to have been involved in the whiskey trading period and was one of the first settlers in the village of Fort Macleod when it was established in 1874.

13. This spread, owned by E.T. Cummins and John Morgan, was known as the Ballybrach Ranch.

14. This was William Berry who ranched on the old Indian farm with his two sons, George and S.W. Their cattle brand was 45 on the left hip while for horses it was 8P on the right shoulder. Mr. and Mrs. Berry settled on the ranch in June 1886 and in later years they bought a hardware store in Pincher Creek.

15. Lewis H. Hunter was the accountant and bookkeeper for the Hudson's Bay Co.

16. Duncan John Campbell was one of the most successful entrepreneurial businessmen in Fort Macleod. Besides being the postmaster, he was the sheriff, an auctioneer, insurance agent, and dealt in real estate.

17. Henry Samuel Casey was born in Colborne, Ont., in 1848, and in 1886 he was appointed an Inspector in the North-West Mounted Police. This position carried the honorary title of "Captain." After his basic training, he was at Edmonton from 1887 to 1889, at Lethbridge, 1889-92, and Fort Macleod, 1892-98. He then went to Prince Albert where he served until his death in 1904.

18. Johnny Franklin was one of the famous bronc busters of southern Alberta. Born in Texas in 1863, he came north with a cattle herd over the Chisholm Trail and worked for ranchers in Montana. He came to Alberta in 1889, breaking horses on the Strong Ranch. He took over as foreman for Patrick and Davis in 1894 and later bought their herd. In the late 1890s he bought the Tommy Atkins ranch, south of Fort Macleod, where he raised purebred Percheron horses. Later, he moved to another ranch south of Brocket. During these years, he was famous for his ability as a rider. He took part in one of Alberta's first rodeos and was a judge of the bucking horse competitions at the first Calgary Stampede in 1912. He died in 1946.

19. Michael J. Holland had a ranch in the Porcupine Hills. His horse brand was an F on the left hip. Interesting, in 1891, he did not have a cattle brand, supporting Gardiner's comments about his lifestyle as a rancher. Holland·was a member of the North Fork polo team.

20. Among the Dunbar family was James Dunbar and wife, and their son Samuel with his wife Eliza. James and his wife had come west from Guelph, Ont., in 1882 and settled on their ranch a short time later. When Samuel married in 1890, he moved to his own homestead but when the elder Dunbar became ill, he rented to a ranch near his parents. When they sold out to Gardiner, the parents lived with Samuel for a short time but they moved to Fort Macleod where the elder Dunbars died a short time later. Samuel then returned to the Porcupine Hills where he died in 1905. His widow returned to Fort Macleod where she operated a boarding house for many years.

21. The Walrond Ranch was known locally as the "Waldron." It was formed by British interests in 1883, with Sir John Walrond-Walrond being the principal shareholder. Dominion Veterinarian Surgeon Duncan McEachran was its general manager and was unpopular with some people because of his aggressive attitude. The ranch had a vast lease on the west side of the Porcupine Hills where McEachran carried on an incessant battle to keep settlers off their land. The ranch suffered badly in the disastrous winter of 1906-07 and a year later the shareholders sold the company to Pat Burns.

22. John Black arrived in Fort Macleod in 1884 where he was store manager for I.G. Baker & Co. When the company was taken over by the Hudson's Bay Co., Black joined that firm and remained with them until he opened his own store. He was an extremely popular man who was known for his sense of humour. He died in 1899 at the age of forty-seven.

23. The incident was described as follows in the Dec. 6, 1895 edition of *The Macleod Gazette*. "On Friday last, Mr. John Lamar, foreman of the Walrond ranch, shot Mr. Gilbert McKay. Two shots, the only ones fired, took effect, one hitting McKay in the stomach and the other in the shoulder. As soon as the shooting took place, Mr. Lamar rode into town, sent out Dr. Kennedy and then gave himself up to the police . . ." L.V. Kelly, in *The Range Men* (Toronto: Coles, 292-93), states: "McKay became obsessed with the belief that Lamar was opening and reading or else delaying certain personal correspondence of his, and he voiced his complaint very loudly, working himself eventually to such a towering rage that he rode out to the Waldron Ranch with the expressed intention of shooting Lamar on sight. Arriving there he called for Lamar, who stepped unarmed form the house, and was immediately made the subject of a most bitter verbal attack, which culminated in a demand that Lamar get his gun and shoot the question out to a satisfactory finish. Lamar tried to pacify the inflamed McKay, but only aroused him to more bitter invective, so bitter in fact that Lamar lost his temper also and repaired indoors, reappearing with his guns strapped on. McKay, seeing this, drew his revolver to shoot, but before he could level the weapon Lamar had drawn and fired twice, striking his opponent in arm and body and toppling him out of his saddle. First aid was rendered the unfortunate searcher for trouble by cowboys who came running up, and Lamar went to town to give himself up to the authorities, who, upon hearing the true facts of the case, decided that McKay had received that for which he had looked, and that no prosecution would be necessary."

Index